RESILIENT MIND

RESILIENT MIND

The 3-Step Process of Renewing the Mind

Dr. Raúl Sánchez

Copyright © 2025 Raúl Sánchez. All Rights Reserved. No portion of this book may be reproduced, stored in a retrieval system, or transmitted in any form or by any means—electronic, mechanical, photocopy, recording, scanning, or other—except for brief quotations in critical reviews or articles without the prior permission of the author.

Published by Game Changer Publishing

Paperback ISBN: 978-1-965653-67-8

Hardcover ISBN: 978-1-965653-68-5

Digital ISBN: 978-1-965653-69-2

Except where noted, Bible quotations are taken from the King James Version.

The Holy Bible, English Standard Version® (ESV®)

Copyright © 2001 by Crossway, a publishing ministry of Good News Publishers.

All rights reserved.

"Thank you" by Ray H. Boltz © 1988

Songwriters: Dido Armstrong/Paul Herman

"Thank You" lyrics © Universal Music- Z Tunes LLC

www.GameChangerPublishing.com

DEDICATION

*For our children: Tyler & Alyseia, Terrence & Melody, Tavian, and Valencia.
For our children's children. For the love of my life, Stacey.*

*In loving memory of
Aunt Gerri
Ruth Castillo
Margret & Leo Fish
Valencia & Ray Fife
Aunt Peg (Margaret) Heiland
Fran Fish*

READ THIS FIRST

Just to say thanks for buying and reading my book,
I would like to give you a free inspirational video
to help you get a jump on your climb!

You may also join our free community to be
included in our movement!

Scan the QR Code Here:

RESILIENT MIND

THE 3-STEP PROCESS OF RENEWING THE MIND

Dr. Raúl Sánchez

www.GameChangerPublishing.com

ACKNOWLEDGMENTS

Appreciation of the Living Legacy We Have Built Together

Stacey, I owe you! You have always been the spark in my step, the joy in my smile, and the peach of my eye. It is so amazing to look back and see our 39 years of maturity, individually and as our one-flesh team!

To say that you are my greatest earthly blessing is a fact. Yes, I have a lot of earthly blessings, including Herlinda, Grandma Ruth, Aunt Gerri, Jerry, Fran, Edie, all my siblings, my in-laws, and each of our kids and grandkids! However, only you have led me to the Lord, our savior, Jesus Christ of Nazareth. You were prophesied to be Deborah—a judge, a sweet honeybee, a humble warrior, an incredibly honest friend, and so much more. I have always said you are a Silent Lioness, that quiet killer that suffocates with kindness. You, through the guidance of the Holy Spirit, pulled me out of my *mental prison* until I could actually see that which had me shackled. Only then was I able to see that it was Jesus who allowed me to see you. The protector in me jumped at the opportunity to love and protect you—but it was you who protected me from my own *mental prison* with Christ's agape love!

My gratitude is to you for showing me the Jesus in you in such a way that pulled me out of my *mental prison*; then Jesus inclined my heart to hear, see, feel, and finally accept love! Lastly, we repeated this process with my grandma Ruth, my mom Herlinda, and each of my siblings: Norma, Ruben, Eugene, Yolanda, and Andrea. You exposed my entire family genogram to the "light that shines into the darkness and the darkness comprehended it not" (John 1:5). Jesus knew that I would accept the light from you, and my family would accept that glorious light from me so that we could see and comprehend the light of the *finished* work of Jesus Christ on that old rugged tree! I will forever be indebted to you, Stacey, because it all started with that Deborah spirit birthed into you that you have cultivated with the agape love of Jesus Christ.

To our children, Tyler and Alyseia, Terrence and Melody, Tavian, and Valencia, I say thank you! Thank you for the ability to lead, serve, and learn from each of you. I promise you that I would not be as resilient, as congruent, as contagious, as dedicated to Christ Jesus, and as driven to establish, keep, preserve, and pass down our *Living Legacy* without each of you walking behind me!

Ever since I heard the Phillips, Craig, and Dean song "I Want to Be Just Like You" in 1994 (Capitol CMG Publishing, Heaven Networks LLC), I have been keenly aware that our children only become what they see *behaviorally* at home. Therefore, I thank you with all that I am that the Lord God of Heaven and Earth, through the *finished* work of Jesus Christ, trusted me to steward each of you! I am forever grateful for the opportunity to walk in front of you, knowing that you are watching, learning, and mimicking every move I make to level up where I left off. Never ever forget:

"There's

To Be Great: When You Feel Like It And When You Don't!"™

CONTENTS

Introduction   xiii

PART I
RENEWING YOUR PERSPECTIVE

1. My Mental Prison   3
2. It's Positive   11
3. Breaking the Chains   23
4. Summary: Renewing Your Perspective   31

PART II
MOVING TOWARD UNCERTAINTY

5. Resilience   39
6. Attempting Resiliency   47
7. Christmas With Tyler   55
8. Resiliency Has Feet   61
9. Confronting Limiting Beliefs   67
10. Summary: Moving Toward Uncertainty   75

PART III
FINDING WHAT'S AWESOME ABOUT THAT (WAAT)

11. Let Go to Grow   83
12. Chasing Down the Dream   87
13. Finding the Hand of God   95
14. Summary: Finding What's Awesome About That (WAAT)   99

INTRODUCTION

This is the foundational verse that changed my life on so many levels.

And be not conformed to this world: but be ye transformed by the renewing of your mind, that ye may prove what is that good, and acceptable, and perfect, will of God.
(Romans 12:2) KJV

RESILIENT MIND: The 3-Step Process of Renewing The Mind, is part of a 3-book series on building resiliency through renewing. In this first book, we are only scratching the surface of how dynamic, deeply moving, and incredibly metamorphic this process of renewing becomes.

We have a Living Legacy Coaching program where we walk people through 12 pillars of Resiliency—one per month. We attack the process daily, and it is our hope to make positive and truly metamorphic, lasting change every month.

The process described in Romans 12:2 contains three parts. Each part is significant in its own right and must be fully embraced to progress to the next. I don't view them as strictly linear; rather, they are interwoven. One can move from one stage to the next without fully mastering the current level.

In part II or part III, it is expected that you will encounter another level of awareness from a hindsight perspective from part I. You are able to implement the new hindsight awareness into the current part II or III to continue renewing more thoroughly. The process is dynamic. Hence, it gives you the ability to renew your mind weekly—if not even more rapidly.

Let's take a brief walk through the three-step process here.

Part 1: RENEW YOUR PERSPECTIVE:
"And be not conformed to this world."
(Romans 12:2)

I. Do not conform to the world.

Let us break down the meaning of "And be not *conformed* unto this *world:*" "conform," Strong's G4964, *syschēmatizō*—to conform one's self (i.e., one's mind and character) to another's pattern (fashion one's self to); to copy. Merriam-Webster's Dictionary defines the word "conform" as follows:

1. to give the same shape, outline, or contour to; bring into harmony or accord; intransitive verb

2. to be similar or identical; to be in agreement or harmony with/to

2. a) to be obedient or compliant with;

2. b) to act in accordance with prevailing standards or customs.

The meaning of the word "world," Strong's G165, *aiōn*—forever, an unbroken age, perpetuity of time, eternity; the world, the universe; period of time; evermore; a messianic period.

Stop copying the world. Stop trying to be like everyone else. This is

Introduction

more than a call to stop copying the behaviors of others. It also means to stop copying the way they think, the way they solve problems, the way they manage their emotions, their patterns of thinking, behaving, and feeling. It's hard to be who you are uniquely called to become if you always follow the crowd. "I praise you [God!], for I am fearfully and wonderfully made [by You!]" (Psalm 139:14) KJV.

In short, to *conform* means to *"adopt the form of those around you."* So our Romans 12:2 call is to ***"be not conformed to this world"*** and thus to ensure that our ability to renew our mind stands upon the foundation that we are called to be different from those around us. We are to stand out from the crowd by simply not adopting the form of those around us. We are called to be unique, separated from the status quo of just blending in, just existing, just being in the crowd and blindly following without any critical thinking, and especially without considering the Hand of God to move the heavens on Earth for us; for you!

You are encouraged to be aware of times in your story when you were conforming and when you were not. Consider the significant struggles in that tension to walk in the comfort of conforming versus the uncertainty of blazing a new uncharted trail and waiting for the Hand of the Lord to guide you by commanding his guardian angels' charge over you!

Do you realize that you have ten unique fingerprints endowed to you by our creator? There are an estimated seven-plus billion people walking the face of our beautiful Earth and yet not one can match *your* created fingerprints. Stop copying other people and start conforming to the image created for you to walk into. That is your calling, your creativity, your destiny. No one before you and nobody after you will be able to match your unique fingerprints. You are literally one of a kind in the entire universe.

Let us agree that you will devote your first step in Renewing Your Perspective to seeing yourself as God intended. No, not as you are. As God intended. You have unique gifts, talents, and offerings that you bring to all those who know, trust, and love you. Renewing Your Perspective starts now, and it starts here!

ACTION STEP I: RENEW YOUR PERSPECTIVE!

Introduction

PART II: MOVING TOWARD UNCERTAINTY:

"...be ye transformed by the renewing of your mind...."
(Romans 12:2)

II. Be transformed by the renewal of your mind.

"Be Ye Transformed"

Merriam-Webster's Dictionary defines "transform" as a verb meaning to change in composition, appearance, character, or condition. It also refers to mathematical and genetic transformations. In its intransitive form, it means to undergo change. The Bible, from Strong's G3326, states that *Transform* is translated from "metamorphoō"—to change into another form, to transform, to transfigure.

"Renewing"

The Bible, from Strong's G342, states that Renewing is translated from "anakaninōsis," which means a renewal, renovation, and complete change for the better.

"Mind"

The Bible, from Strong's G3563, states that the Mind is translated from "nous" (noose), the intellect, i.e., mind (divine or human; in thought, feeling, or will); by implication, meaning mind, understanding.

> I. the *mind*, comprising alike the faculties of perceiving and understanding and those feeling, judging, determining;
>
> a) the intellectual faculty, the understanding;
>
> b) reason in the narrower sense, as the capacity for spiritual truth, the higher powers of the soul, the faculty of perceiving divine things, of recognizing goodness and of hating evil;

Introduction

c) the power of considering and judging soberly, calmly, and impartially;

II. a particular mode of thinking and judging, i.e., thoughts, feelings, purposes, desires.

For the purpose of this book, based on 25 years of clinical psychology experience—and the direction from the Bible during these experiences as a Christian Psychologist—we have used the action steps of Renewing, Moving, and Finding to represent our standing verse, Romans 12:2.

To be transformed means you are becoming a new you. By allowing a renewing of the way you think, process information, problem-solve, and adapt to novel information, you literally are becoming—transforming—into a new and improved *you*.

Interestingly, this new and improved you is actually your original programming that somehow got lost. It is who our Lord created you to be. Once you have learned to stop conforming to what people say you are or what the pressure of loved ones leads you to believe about yourself, you are able to transform into your original design. This occurs as you stop believing all those old thought patterns that have imprisoned you: all the labels you have accepted about yourself, all fears that you have been unable to shake that grew out of uncertainty, doubts, and shame. Your old thought patterns corner you into a holding pattern that drains your mental energy. When you are mentally worn out—mentally stuck—you feel imprisoned. When stuck in this cycle of thinking that you have become addicted to, your enemy tells you this position of failure is actually you. But it is only the program on the mental TV that you left on. It is the last commercial jingle that is running through your head on repeat. When you change this habitual jingle, you can begin to transform who you believe you are.

"Wait—what!?" you say. Oh, you have tried to change these old thinking patterns so many times before! So now you feel you want to put down this book. Believe me, I get it! But it's different now. The difference is we are not going to sit around and fret about any previous attempts that crashed and failed. Today is a new day! We are going to MOVE.

Did you know that physically moving forward toward a known anxiety or fear literally dissipates the anxiety and fear response? Conversely, a physical withdrawal continues to invite the anxiety and fear response.[1]

Therefore, your new job is to *move* toward the uncertainty, whatever makes fear grow in you, because your physical movement makes the fear conform to reality. The reality is you are only afraid because you haven't been there before. It is new to you. You are uncertain.

This is called *anticipatory anxiety*. You are anticipating being anxious. As you move toward uncertainty, you see positive opportunities that you could not see before. Your new movement now reinforces your renewed perspective! The winning is in the MOVING, my friend. So today, we *MOVE!*

ACTION STEP II: MOVE TOWARD UNCERTAINTY!

PART III: FINDING *WHAT'S AWESOME ABOUT THAT* (WAAT):

"...that ye may prove what is that good, and acceptable, and perfect, will of God."
(Romans 12:2)

III. You may prove what the will of God is!

Test what God says about you. One who is *born again* has a new mind. Go! See and believe what God has for you. You can see it first, then believe. Or you may also believe it first, then go look to see it manifest. God loves bold faith and God manifests at the speed of your faith so long as what you are asking aligns with His sovereign will.

What is so amazing is that our Heavenly Father has a Will specifically designed for you, yet He wants you to test it to "prove" that it is

---

1. Huberman, A. (2021) Episode 49: Erasing fear & traumas based on the modern neuroscience of fear. *Huberman Lab Podcast*, 14 December.

Introduction

genuine. The word "prove" is translated as "Dokimazo" from Strong's Concordance #1381, and it means to test, examine, and scrutinize to make sure that something is genuine.

Did you know that, in their training to recognize counterfeit U.S. currency notes (money), the staff of the Federal Reserve literally study and memorize the *genuine* notes? Thus, they hold the authentic currency and study it intimately. Then, when they see a counterfeit, they see it for what it is immediately by testing and proving it against what they know to be the authentic, the real, the genuine truth.

Think about it: studying counterfeit money to identify what makes it fake is a waste of time because each counterfeit note differs, making it a constant game of tag with counterfeiters who continually change their tactics.

Instead, logging a ton of time hanging out with the *genuine notes* means your habits are formed with the true U.S. currency, so any attempt to bend the truth will stick out to you like a sore thumb.

In this same way, staying close to our Heavenly Father in prayer, worship and praise singing, and studying the scriptures to find out how and where the Lord is leading you means when you feel that true and genuine peace of God, then you truly know that you know that it is as real and genuine as touching your own face! Stop chasing fads and trends and following crowds from back in the line only to wait your turn to get up to the front and then realize you have been played. Stop studying counterfeits. Start testing and approving that which is good, acceptable, and perfect will of God for you and for such a time as this!

How do we test and approve God, you ask? Well, I am not certain, but for twenty years, I have taught people to test the hand of God by asking this one question: *"What's Awesome About That* (WAAT)?" Here is an example of how it all works.

After being stuck in a situation and feeling the best way out is to give up, give in, or quit. You worked hard to renew your perspective and finally found a new perspective to get yourself unstuck from this situation. Now, you are starting to move in a new direction, one that makes you very uncomfortable, and the same feelings of wanting to

Introduction

give up, give in, or quit resurface. You are now feeling very stupid because "I am stuck if I do and stuck if I don't."

So, let us deploy the WAAT question. "What is Awesome About That" in the new situation you find yourself in? You were stuck and wanted to quit. You renewed your perspective and also decided to move toward the thing that had you stuck, and after freeing yourself once, you suddenly feel like you are getting stuck again. So, where is a WAAT moment when you feel stuck again after moving? Well, one WAAT is that you are no longer stuck in the same place. Another is that you literally were moving. Another is that if you got unstuck once, isn't it more likely that you can get unstuck again? Another is to let us renew our perspective here in step III and find that we probably are not truly stuck. Rather, we need to gain more tools as this is new territory for you. The list goes on and on and on. One of the greatest testimonies from my coaching clients is, "I wanted to punch you because you kept asking me for a WAAT, and I knew you wouldn't give me one until I found it myself—and it worked!"

Talk is cheap. Actions speak louder than words. Actions lead to finding, and it's the testing and proving that leads us to those WAAT moments during the most difficult challenges in life. When we find a WAAT moment within what sucks, then what can stop us? Not today, Satan! I found another WAAT moment!

This entire Renewing The Mind process (steps I-III), is what we call **"12:2ING."** It's the process of *actively* Renewing your perspective, MOVING Toward Uncertainty, and Finding the WAAT moments in every situation of life. It is in attacking this process that we build a RESILIENT MIND!

Action step III: FIND WAAT Moment(s) in Every Situation!

PART I

RENEWING YOUR PERSPECTIVE

(I) And be not conformed to this world,
(II) but be ye transformed by the renewing of your mind,
(III) that ye may prove what is that good, and acceptable,
and perfect, will of God.
(Romans 12:2, KJV)

ACTION STEP I: RENEW YOUR PERSPECTIVE!

"I will not let anyone walk through my mind with their dirty feet."
– Mahatma Gandhi

1

MY MENTAL PRISON

Let me begin by telling you a bit of my story to show you how I learned what I have learned about taking steps to Renew, Move, and Find!

THE CHASE

In the summer of 1986, I was 15 years old and had been invited to a swimming party with an extended group of friends. I had been introduced to a young lady named Stacey. I inquired about her later that day at a different friend's house. I was informed that she had a boyfriend and that there was no reason to try to talk with her because she was locked in with her boyfriend.

Later that fall semester, I had tenth-grade Algebra with Stacey, and she was even more attractive once I got to know her personality. She was sweet, calm, emotionally stable (not at all moody), and laughed at my humor, but she would not flirt. She was smart: she asked questions in class. I could have cheated off her tests if she had complied. Since I couldn't get her to pay attention to me, I devised a plan.

Our entire math pod area bottle-necked, with everyone heading out the doors to the main hallway. I always found a way to stand right behind her. But instead of trying to talk to her, I simply gave her a "flat tire." This was accomplished by stepping on the heel of her shoe when it was her planted foot. She lifted her foot, causing her shoe to slip off the back of her foot. She then had to stop and fix her shoe. This was my plan to get her to stop, so I had her attention to talk with her.

Initially, it didn't work! But I grew on her in an annoying kind of way, and I was able to talk to her during a very short hallway walk. My plan was only 50% productive. It allowed me to get her attention. But she still did not give me her number. When a seemingly well-thought-out plan fails, it is great to review and adjust your strategy. I leaned on a mutual friend to get her number.

I started calling her several times per week and just talking about Algebra questions. Then, general school questions. Then, questions about her being a football cheerleader and myself being a football player. Eventually, I was brave enough to ask questions about her homecoming plans. She mentioned possibly going with her current boyfriend, but she didn't know for sure because he went to a different school, and he had not asked her yet.

I had an opportunity! I made a plan. I started asking about her friends and who they were going to homecoming with. I started talking about mutual friends, the possibility of a large group of friends going together, and how much fun it would be for all of us. She was calm, stable, and not at all swayed by my storytelling abilities. Although I am not one to give up, I honestly thought about it.

Instead, I called her after school. I simply said, "Stacey, I have a serious question to ask you. Are you interested?" She said she was. I continued, "I need you to call your boyfriend and tell him you have to break up with him. When he asks why, you simply say, "I'll tell you later." When you are done, call me back, and I'll ask you this very important question."

After about ten minutes, she called me back, and I simply said, "Now that you are single, will you be my homecoming date?"

Without a moment of hesitation, she replied, "Yes." Obviously, she had a hunch, which was the question I had asked her before.

I have done a lot of "outside-the-box" type thinking and behaving in my life, and most of the time, it has failed me. On occasion, when my crazy line of thinking lands me a successful moment in time, I don't typically get too excited. I actually have a list of other options. I have always been considered an idea machine and a dreamer. In this particular case, although I fully expected Stacey to say, "Yes," when she did not hesitate, I literally jumped up off the ground and landed face-down on my waterbed in utter joy! Still, I was actually shocked that she wanted to give me a chance to take her out on homecoming night.

It was that moment in time when your brain realizes that the functional work to get here was all worth it. As a result, you are more likely to take another risk like this one. This moment is like my real-life golf game. I look past the 90% of bad shots and absolutely savor the 10% of amazing shots—like when my drive went 336 yards on a course in Okoboji, Iowa, and my son, Terrence, was there to see it unfold! Oh, and I videoed the range finder distance to the pin before my second shot for my oldest son, Tyler. Gotcha! In life, we far too often focus on the negative, the wrongs, the issues that offend us, the seemingly sticky stuff we cannot shake off. Then we set up camp in these positions, and it suddenly becomes our life's work to carry those burdens and tell stories about them to explain to others why we remain in captivity. And yet, those situations (90% in this example) are only meant to teach and not to become a *foundation* upon which we *build our life!*

Instead, our minds naturally move toward things our body knows we believe in. We naturally avoid things we do not believe in. Here is where the rubber meets the road. We get what we *truly believe!*

Let me set some parameters because, obviously, even with the True Belief that you can fly, jumping from a roof is not going to end well. First, I am speaking about renewing your perspective in social settings, in relationships, and situations such as an audition, job interview, etc. Secondly, there is something very real and tangible, like the HPA axis, about our mind-body connection and how it knows what you truly want and believe—not just what you say you want or believe!

The HPA Axis is the Hypothalamic – Pituitary – Adrenal axis (HPA). Together, these three organs release hormones that either raise or lower the body's cortisol levels. This is the system that sparks fight–

flight–freeze–fawn. This neuroendocrine system senses nervous system stimulation and responds accordingly to your true belief about that specific situation.[1]

Sure, you are all in and going for it, giving your 110 percent. However, only you and your gut-brain know you literally believe you will fail. If you have listened to me before, then you know the importance I place on the concept of mental, physical, and spiritual congruence! In short, it may look like a near miss at your top goal in life, but internally, you already knew—you had already accepted the fact that you would miss the mark. Your mind-body connection was not in congruence as foretold by your HPA axis and the amount of stress hormones released in the bloodstream. This is what I am speaking of when I say *True Belief*: when you know that you know the Lord has covered you *"with favor as a shield"* (Psalms 5:12 KJV).

In my case, I truly believed Stacey would say yes! I could feel her getting more interested—even if it was only out of curiosity (or perhaps charity, haha!). I did not spend any time in prayer at that time, as that was not something I thought about, let alone practiced. But I felt it deep within me. I was fully released in my gut that this was what I wanted, and I believed I was going to be successful.

I have never thought to ask Stacey why she did what I asked and why she said yes to me for homecoming in 1986. So, guess what? I asked her while writing this section of the book, and her astounding answer was [*drum roll*]:

"Well, obviously, I wanted to. I liked you!"

Boom, baby! Or, as my daughter says when she dominates something, "Boomba—Baam!!"

I can still feel that explosive moment in 1986 when she said, "Yes," and my body exploded off the ground, and I landed face-first on my waterbed. This is the culmination of a *True Belief!*

---

1. Cleveland Clinic, "What Is the HPA Axis?," *Cleveland Clinic*, accessed 2024, [https://my.clevelandclinic.org/health/body/hypothalamic-pituitary-adrenal-hpa-axis] (https://my.clevelandclinic.org/health/body/hypothalamic-pituitary-adrenal-hpa-axis).

OF THE WORLD

We went to homecoming and had a great time with all our friends. Stacey's parents hosted an after-party where we played fun games. After a week of talking, I asked Stacey if she wanted to "date me" and not just be a homecoming couple. She said yes. I visited her at her job, Orange Julius, and she visited me where I worked at my grandma's restaurant, Ruth's Cosina.

Her parents had a rule: if we were going out on a date on the weekend, then I had to go with Stacey and her parents to church that prior Sunday. I did this for as long as we dated. At first, it was simply fulfilling an assignment. I asked Stacey a lot of questions. She never wavered on her faith in Jesus Christ. She calmly explained what she knew and often asked her parents for a way to explain it to me more.

I had a negative reputation. I was "of the world." I conformed to what I thought I was supposed to do. I did what I saw other teen males do. I looked out only for myself. I dated girls for what I wanted physically or needed emotionally. I had heard growing up that it was a "dog-eat-dog world," so I ate.

Stacey was completely different. People warned her not to date me. I wasn't good for her, they said. She could do better than me. Stacey was and is strong-minded. She did hear their warnings, and she often told me about them. All I could say was, "Watch me because I'm different now."

Stacey had the peace of God that the Bible speaks about. I could tell, and it drove me to ask questions and find out more about her faith in Jesus Christ. The more I knew, the more I felt like I didn't belong.

All of my life, I've seen failed relationships in every direction I have looked. I didn't understand self-limiting beliefs at that time, but they indeed wrecked my family, myself included. So, as I got more transparent with Stacey, she began to break down my long-held generational lies. She was literally tearing down my truths about myself, my family, and my faith just by asking, "What if that isn't God's plan for you?"

My mentor, pastor Francis Frangipane, called these generational lies a "house made of cards." He was my pastor and mentor while at the University of Iowa from 1994–1998. Indeed, these lies in my head were just that. As Stacey continued to dig deeper into my life, in 1986, she uncovered a lot of my mental prisons of unbelief: thoughts like, *God can—but not for me.* I tried to push Stacey away by telling her huge family secrets of abuse, neglect, abandonment, and even our trauma histories. When the truth of my painful history didn't scare her, I sometimes exaggerated the story to push her away from these deep emotional pains. However, it all continued to build more heartfelt compassion in her, and she wanted to pray for me and my extended family. She kept pressing in and took me on a deep dive into the fallacies upon which I was standing behind a wall of self-protection.

Interestingly, people often build a wall of self-protection to keep other people out, to stop the bleeding, so to speak. But that also stops our healing! Healing comes only through sharing the pain. When another human shows compassion and understanding of our pain and why we feel the way we do, it allows us to SHED—let go of the pain. This is the irony of those efforts of self-protection that I call a mental prison!

So, I did the only thing I knew to do when facing huge pain. I lied. I told her that I was a cocaine addict and a drug dealer. I told her lies that I was in a drug dealing ring with my father figure, Jose, and we were bad dudes. Stay away! I was a wanted felon and could be arrested any day now, so our dating relationship was over!

I didn't know what was happening then. Knowing what I know now, I realize I didn't have an ounce of True Belief that I was good enough for Stacey. Here are my perspectives and conclusions:

"I do not deserve you."

"I do not deserve the love you give to me."

"I do not have the capacity to love you the way that you love me or the way that you deserve to be loved."

"I do not deserve a loving and forgiving God."

In every way, I was emotionally exposed and incredibly vulnerable. Stacey was looking right through me. All of me. She had already seen and experienced the free-loving, creative prankster—the authentic me. I did not realize that I had given Stacey the key to my inner self, the hidden and protected part *no one* had ever seen before. It was a part that even I was afraid to admit to because an angry, aggressive, wounded WARRIOR would emerge and fight his way back to a self-protected bunker to hide safely in armor. My armor allowed me to keep my mask up. That feeling of self-protection allowed me not to worry that I would be left behind again. Abandoned again. Broken again, ultimately rejected and unwanted.

Still, Stacey's sense of peace, calm, and stability kept me close. Typically, when I push someone away, I hit emotional buttons with big haymaker knockout punches. The people I lashed out at would very quickly develop anger toward me. That made it easy for us to mutually decide it was time to end the relationship. I was an expert in the art of self-protection. I was renowned for my ability to push haymaker buttons on people by cutting them down and exposing insecurities to make them cry. Then they would leave me. I wouldn't have to be the only one to want to break up. No, I didn't like doing that, but, in all honesty, it was easier than confronting my own mental prison!

"Sweet Stacey" (as she was called by her friends) didn't accept being rejected by me. Instead, she pressed in harder and prayed for me. She gave me scriptures explaining that there is literally nothing under the sun that can make the Son of God cast you out from his unconditional love. She shared with me that we are all loved unconditionally by God by this covering called grace. It is a free gift, like a get-out-of-jail card, that you cannot earn with good behavior or lose with bad behavior. It is simply always present.

But like any gift, you have to unwrap it, accept it, and possess it as your own. It is your own FREE GIFT CALLED GRACE!

I realize that this may make my man card null and void, but I cried. I cried like never before. I was shedding so much emotional pain, injury, suffering, and the heavy lies I'd heard about me. This shedding was even exposing my own negative self-talk. When we face so much hate about us for our entire lives, even our own words begin to wreck us.

The last time I was physically abused was at 13 years old. I was beaten like an unwanted dog. At 14, I fought back. I got the best of him and threw my intoxicated father figure down the stairs. This meant I was free from any physical abuse for about two years. But my mind was playing past statements, my own words, back at me. It was a broken record of hate, now in my voice, verbally abusing myself by mimicking what others said about me for years. It was as if I was confessing stuff. I needed to, but didn't know it. I didn't know that I carried it or that it was something I had the power to shed.

My relationship with Stacey grew emotionally and spiritually. In fact, this is when I realized that I am a hugger—or at least that I love being hugged. It's like I literally began *accepting* a hug from someone rather than passively allowing it. Allowing and *accepting* are worlds apart! I wanted to know more, to read and understand the Bible more. I wanted more. I wanted to study the scriptures more. I wanted to talk about these heavy things more. I wanted to pull more out of my emotional backpack and share more with Stacey. I didn't know when or how. But I wanted more. I literally felt like I was becoming a new man.

2

IT'S POSITIVE

"Well, it's positive."

I immediately felt a sense of relief and said, "Yes."

She reacted. "Do you even know what that means?"

I shrugged my shoulders and quietly said, "Um, you have good news for us?"

Throwing her hands up in the air as if I just hit a game-winning 3-pointer, she said, "That means the pregnancy test is positive. You are about to become a father."

We were both 16 years old. It was 1987, the spring semester of our high school sophomore year. We had been dating for six months and were at Planned Parenthood in separate meeting rooms.

"I'm going to be a dad? I'm going to be a dad?" I just keep asking this question again. Suddenly, I heard her voice again.

"Do you want to hear the statistics again?"

Obviously, I wasn't all there. I was lost in thought. *How do I proceed? How do I earn enough cash? How do I stay in school?* I fluctuated in and out of my prefrontal cortex line of thinking—where I am physically present at the moment—and into my deep, lost thoughts of deciding my next sequential order of steps.

The clinic counselor, an employee of Planned Parenthood, ran through some stats of kids born to teen parents and the life opportunities and success differences between poor teen parents and married adult parents. She spoke about the options: abortion and adoption. All I could think about was becoming a dad and the possibility of not being able to parent my child. I realize how ridiculous this sounds, but from a very early age, I would typically think, *When I have kids, I'm going to be the best dad ever!* Most kids typically think, *I can't wait until I can get out of this house.* But I was looking forward to developing dad skills so I could give my kids a much better opportunity than I was living. I promise you that I wasn't planning on having a child yet. I wasn't prepared to have a child. It was not my or Stacey's intent. I realize it seems like people in this position often ask, "How did this happen?" Well, that wasn't me or Stacey. I was more focused on figuring out how to move forward. My core motivation—my fight mode—kicks in when people throw stats in my face and tell me 'I can't' before giving me a chance to step up and try.

I do not care who *you* are or what some numbers say about me. I know that I am a MEX-*I*-CAN! The counselor showed me pamphlet after pamphlet about abortion and about adoption, although it clearly wasn't my choice. She wanted me to be fully informed before talking with Stacey. What I continually heard through my emotional filters was, "You are not good enough for your child!"

My definition of being racist is this: After looking at me, someone shows me statistics that somehow include me—although I wasn't tested or given a chance—then argues in my face that someone else's numbers say, "You can't!"

My response? "Watch me!"

When we were both released, Stacey and I sat in the car and talked for a long time. Stacey was more upset about the push to abort, and I was stuck on what I interpreted as "YOU are not good enough." Stacey cried and cried, which made me cry, too. I held her hand and told her it would be okay. I told her we were together and we could fight through anything.

As I look back on this episode, I find it interesting how I was strong for her but not for myself. We decided that we would talk with Norma, my older sister. She was the only person I trusted enough to call us out of school and get us appointments at Planned Parenthood. Stacey dropped me off at my house. We agreed that we would think about how and when to present the news to her parents and my mom. We agreed that we would hold tight until I got a second job before we broke the news.

Alone at my house, panic began to set in. I began to wonder, "What if I am *not* good enough?" Then, I began to self-protect. The emotional pain of not being wanted as a son hit home. My biological dad committed suicide after I was born. He was an alcoholic. To this day, I have no way of knowing what his thought-life, his mindset, or his daily agenda was like. All I know is that I am his baby, the last child he fathered. The straw that broke the camel's back.

Once emotional pain hits home, all of us go back into self-protection mode. I had no clear idea what hit me. I had gone from being a strong presence with Stacey ("We can do this, babe!") to "I am afraid that I will also be a failure as a father. Maybe Planned Parenthood's stats were correct? Who am I to argue with the experts and their facts?"

I began to refocus on my selfish dreams. Our team had just finished an undefeated sophomore football season at 10-0! I was a big, tough, fast running back, and my coaches were saying that I could be a full-ride student-athlete (but I had to improve my GPA).

I began to see Stacey and our child as impeding me from my childhood dream of playing college football. I sensed a new motivation to fight, but only for me. I started to dream again about playing college football or even going pro. If I went pro in football, then I could come back to take care of Stacey and our child, couldn't I? This selfish motivation and self-protection seemed the right way out of the emotional pain.

THE CHRIST-CENTERED RESPONSE TO FEAR

I got a phone call from Stacey only a couple of hours after we left Planned Parenthood. She was crying. I couldn't hear what she was attempting to explain through her tears and pain. She was saying, "I'm sorry, I'm sorry, but my mom just knows."

I started to get angry at how she broke our promise to wait to tell. Then Stacey said, "The Holy Spirit told my mom!"

I was nowhere near their faith and their trust in the power of the Lord. I said what you may be thinking: "You're joking?"

Then Stacey explained. "Mom was upstairs when I came home. I went straight to my bedroom. I hid in my closet and cried. Mom just came downstairs and said, 'You are pregnant, aren't you?'"

Stacey told her mom yes and asked how she knew. Her mom simply answered, "The Holy Spirit told me."

They both cried, and Fran, her mom, just said, "It will all be alright."

Normally, a couple's announcement that they are expecting a child is one of the greatest moments in their lives. The funny thing about our testimony of this greatest opportunity in life is this: Fran wanted to tell Jerry, Stacey's dad, but she was worried he would be mad at Stacey. So she waited until Jerry was "on the throne." At our house, we would say, "Jerry was taking a dump." Ha ha! Fran waited for him to be locked in and on the toilet, where he would have time to work through any anger he felt. He was also sitting still enough for Fran to talk through it all with him. So they talked and prayed about how the Lord wanted them to proceed—with Stacey, with us, and in this life-altering opportunity of a lifetime for all of us.

Jerry and Fran worked through it as a one-flesh married team (Genesis 1:24).

Then, they spoke with Stacey. As Jerry recalls that day, he walked downstairs to Stacey's bedroom. She heard him and wailed, "Dad, my life is ruined!"

Jerry wisely said, "No, it isn't, honey. It's just different now."

What we decide to call our circumstances has always been, and always will be, a mindset game that wins and loses legacies. Little, subtle things like naming something as "different" versus "ruined" may seem trivial at first. But that moment, multiplied by 365 days, multiplied by 35 years of marriage, allowed us to clearly see the enormous magnitude and wisdom of that "still small voice" called the Holy

Spirit! As Jerry told me years ago while I was playing college football at North Dakota State University, "The Holy Spirit is our Great Equalizer!" The Holy Spirit empowers us to see and say things that are outside our individual magnitude. Listening to the "Comforter" (another name for the Holy Spirit in the Bible) engages the power of Him, who holds the universe in the palm of His hand!

It is unbelievable that the God of the Universe would choose to use me to lead the young lady who changed my life via her personal witness of a personal relationship with Jesus Christ. God assigned her to be the mother of the young son who further changed my heart and soul. Thank you, Jesus!

After they all talked through it as a family, Stacey called me back and informed me that Jerry was picking me up for dinner at their house that same night. He was already on his way! I thought I might get shot, but I knew Jerry didn't own a gun, LOL! Stacey told me that things would be different, but we would be okay.

The conversation in the car was relaxed and mostly a lecture on scriptures. He talked about how—when the world throws stuff at you—the Lord is there to turn it into something good. He did a good job of keeping it low-key and kept me talking with him. During dinner, they got out the Bible and talked about the "betrothal," which is a time of engagement prior to marriage. He talked about the biblical order of marriage and the differences between a covenant marriage blessed by the Lord versus a worldly marriage based on a signed contract that can be easily broken or deemed invalid via annulment. In short, it was a sermonette on marriage, betrothal, and how the Lord works out for our good what could otherwise devastate us (Romans 8:28). There was a lot more dialogue, but nothing of anger, blame, or shame.

During this time, Fran talked about our practical issues. She stated that she would stay home to babysit our child, her grandchild. Stacey would be home after school to watch the baby so Fran could still have her evenings. We talked about my mom's role and my role. As we ate, looked up scriptures, and planned our futures, it was as if Stacey and I would live parallel lives but not yet be introduced into a conversation about marriage specifically. They talked about her goals to go to Evangel University, where Jerry and Fran met and went to college.

That was where Stacey's oldest sister was currently attending. Her middle sister was planning on attending at the end of that school year. Jerry took me home, and we left on a good note with no anger, no blow-ups, and no shame or blame.

It was the craziest thing I had ever experienced in my entire life! Can you even imagine it? Your sweet little 16-year-old Christian daughter is pregnant, and the father is American, of Mexican ethnicity, a non-Christian, residing in a single-parent welfare family with five other kids. Yet, you are calm, organized, trusting God for His provision for your daughter, and able to show the love of Jesus Christ without ever wavering, showing panic, or an ounce of anger. To this day, I praise the Lord God Almighty because, in those moments of discussing consecutive little plans, I learned that I am worthy of the love of Jesus Christ. I know it is odd to speak like this, and until you experience the presence of the Lord upon you, it is almost indescribable. My effort to describe it definitely doesn't do it justice. I simply knew that Stacey and I were going to have the child, stay in school, work our butts off, work on our relationship, and follow the teachings of Jesus Christ. I had a True Belief that we were going to make it!

I hear you ask, "Was it just motivation?" I did not feel as though it was just motivation because it was a deep sense of "Okay, here *we* go," rather than "Can I do this?"

I wasn't as confident about my relationship with Stacey. I still felt unworthy of her and her family. I knew that we would graduate high school and both hit our goals for college. But I was uncertain that Stacey would stay with me. I didn't know why I felt okay then, but I discovered it later. It was the covering of a father! God-fearing fathers provide a spiritual presence that carries confidence and a sense of spiritual authority. It's a deep sense of being protected, covered, or escorted to victory. It was the first time in my life that I felt the spiritual presence of a God-fearing and God-honoring father—even if it was only by proxy of Stacey.

The Bible says, *"The fear of the Lord is the beginning of wisdom, and the knowledge of the Holy One is insight"* (Proverbs 9:10). Jerry Fish was also being covered by his spiritual father, Jesus Christ. As Jesus covered and carried Jerry, Jerry was freed from worrying about himself, about what his friends would think, what his church would say, or how this could tarnish his family's reputation. Instead, he was free to focus only on the purpose for which Stacey and I were put on this Earth and how our little child would be able to follow Jesus from an early age. This is what I call the *Shield of Obedience* (more on this in my third book in this series) that protects our ability to follow the spiritual father, Jesus Christ, on life's most challenging climbs. I mean the huge ones that challenge your faith, all that you stand for, and all that you believe to be true in your life! To Jerry Fish, my earthly spiritual father, I restate to you what I have always stated to you from the moment I heard this worship song while studying at the University of Iowa:

Thank you for giving to the Lord.
I am a life that was changed.
("Thank You For Giving to the Lord," Ray Boltz)

THE PANIC-CENTERED RESPONSE TO FEAR

Do you have children? If yes, then you know the feeling that says, *I hope to give my kids more opportunities than I had.* This was my mom. She has had one of the most difficult lives I have ever encountered in my lifetime! Yes, in my 25 years as a clinical psychologist, Herlinda's story is nothing short of epic, tremendous, and a true outlier!

Yet she still stands, fights, and thrives! She just recently overcame major heart surgery and was even caught by her cardiologist trying to walk-run only two months after full open-heart surgery. I get it! I am cut more from her cloth, praise the Lord, and not from my biological father.

Her story is hers to tell, but let me just say that she is a huge inspiration to anyone who has the opportunity to hear it! I love you, Mom! Nothing can ever repay you for saying "YES" to me, my life, my wife, my kids, and my testimony. You were also a teenage single mom, and even though it was *not* consensual, you still said "YES" to me! Thank you! Thank you! Thank you!

Think for one moment about all the men, women, families, and children that the Lord has placed in my clinical care. Mom, that is possible because you said "YES" to me! What a tremendous blessing you are, Herlinda Sánchez! The love that I have for you can never, ever repay you. Just know that your reward is great as you have stored up treasures in Heaven for your tremendous, selfless love to all of us kids, grandkids, and now great-grandkids! As you have always preached to all of us, Mom, "Te quiero mucho!!!"

It is in your honor that I was even here on Earth to say yes to Stacey as she said "YES" to Tyler! So now you get it.

My mom would not have wanted me to have the life she had as a teen parent. I'm certain she wanted bigger and better things for me.

After my sister heard Stacey's pregnancy test was positive, she couldn't hold that secret for long. She told my mom. When Jerry dropped me off at my house, I went to my room. Moments later, my mom almost busted down my door, screaming at me. In her panic, she shouted, "You are just like your uncles, so you better drop out of school, get a job at IBP, and make enough money for you and the baby because I don't have it for you!"

She was afraid, so she did what I did when I was afraid—she went on the attack. "What about all that talk about you playing college football, about you getting out of Sioux City, about you not wanting to be in the restaurant business, about not being a welfare kid anymore?"

This triggered my panic. I began yelling back. After she left the room, I started feeling that deep, emotional pain of not being wanted, of my mom only keeping me out of obligation, my birth dad not wanting me and taking his own life. These deep emotional pains come on their own, hard, strong, and fast. I struggled to catch my breath as I saw future failures. I saw myself still being stuck and "never amounting to anything," as my stepdad said to me every day.

So, I did what I always did when I was in deep emotional pain: I ran away from the pain. As a young kid, I would ride my bike all day until dark. As I got older, I would go on long runs to get away from the craziness of our house. This time, I went on a long run. During that run, I thought of a brilliant plan: to call my aunt, Esperanza, in Texas and move in with her. Texas is known for football. What better place to escape to and still fight for my childhood dream of playing college football? I would look for a full-ride scholarship since we were on welfare.

I called my aunt, but her number was disconnected. I asked my sister for Aunt Esperanza's current phone number. I was in a desperate, self-protective mode and wanted to run away so I could breathe, think, regroup, and fight for myself. My sister didn't know the new number. I asked my mom, but she refused to help. She told me, "Running away is not what we do."

Then she dropped the bomb: "Running away is what *they* do."

She didn't have to say it, but I felt it. My birth dad quit on himself and all his kids. Today, I finally understand that there was some mental and emotional trauma present, as he ran to alcohol far too often. I do not hold him accountable for anything in my life. I truly believe he was emotionally, mentally, and spiritually broken. I have compassion for my birth dad because to live how he did and to check out of life the way he did tells me he was psychologically injured (PI, similar to a physical disability), completely broken, as in brain-broken. Just like someone breaks a bone and it doesn't work correctly, research is mounting to show that a psychologically injured person doesn't function correctly. I am one of 8 kids on my birth dad's side, and all alone as he was gone.

At 16, I was one of six kids on my mom's side. Three out of four of our fathers had left, and the fourth was in and out of treatment centers for an addiction to pain pills at that point in my life. I knew what Mom meant, and I felt it deep down within me. I wasn't angry—I was speechless. I had an awakening. In my rush to self-protect from my childhood psychological injuries and my current emotional pain, I was ready to run from this new, different season of my life. But with this awakening, I realized that by running away from my personal, emotional pain, I was literally going to infect my child with the same psychological injuries of being abandoned by his biological father.

The pain was real for me. It hit me like a Mike Tyson punch that left me speechless and hyperventilating. I couldn't talk, move, or think. I froze. In a state of panic like that, most people experience the fight-or-flight response that is natural and involuntary. Most believe that they will stand and fight when, in reality, most of us freeze! Despite popular belief that we can only choose between the fight-or-flight options, there is always a third or fourth option: freeze or fawn! Well, that was me. I froze. Then I cried. A lot. I mean, a ton. It was an emotional catharsis, the process of releasing deep, emotional, or repressed pain or feelings. This is sometimes called emotional purging. I didn't know it then, but I was repressing the psychological injuries and pain from early childhood from my biological father's suicide. Then there was the more current emotional pain of having deadbeat father figures.

Now I was feeling that I was about to infect my child with this same lifelong affliction—so difficult to even identify, let alone process or tame. *Wait, am I my father?* That was the all-too-familiar Tyson right hook–left uppercut combo that left me frozen, speechless, tearful, and broken.

This was my whole life in a nutshell. Was I the same as my father? Was I no better than my deadbeat dad figures? Was I that guy? Would I just walk away and abandon my child? It was this parade of self-aware thoughts that brought me a catharsis. Real-life emotional pain makes anyone feel inferior and question their purpose in life. I was only 16. But all I could feel was this: I was at the plate with the bases loaded, and I had to clear the bases of my life, the weight of having failed father figures. Right here and right now, I had to step up to the plate and hit it out of the park with one intentional, fully present, all-in swing. I wanted to be the best dad that ever was to my child! Or I could run away from facing this emotional pain that touched and opened up the old, deep psychological injuries from my biological father. I could try to re-bury it all deeper into my psyche, pretend it never happened, and try to be okay with that. "Fake it until you make it." The junk that just smiles and says, "I'm good, bro." This is it: face the pain and heal, or run away from the pain and pretend my whole life is ahead of me, pain-free.

But I'd never been a pretending or fake kind of guy, so I literally didn't know how to do that—thankfully.

It was here that I asked Jesus Christ to help me, to come into my life and be my Lord and Savior. Some people often say, "Well, you needed something to lean on," or "You really needed a crutch at that time." Justify it as you may. I simply knew that I was not enough and that I hadn't been taught at all how to parent, let alone be the best dad ever. I didn't know about the *how*. But I did know about the *why*! I asked the Lord Jesus Christ into my life because I was broken, lost, stuck, and desperately afraid. I did it by what felt right, but I can't recall the exact prayer today. I assure you that it was far from textbook. I wasn't fully sure of my faith, Christ's resurrection, the historical data, the Holy Spirit, or even how to pray. I knew I desperately needed the presence of God. So, I made some sort of agreement with the Lord. If that was even a possibility, as Stacey had said, I was going after it. I got down on my knees and basically attempted to barter with the Lord. I said something modeled after the Lord's Prayer, the only prayer I knew.

Our Father in Heaven, hallowed be your name. Your kingdom come, your will be done, on Earth as it is in Heaven. Give us this day our daily bread, and forgive us our debts, as we also have forgiven our debtors. And lead us not into temptation but deliver us from evil. (Luke 11:2–4 ESV)

So my prayer went something like this:

Lord God, please forgive me of my sins as I forgive my father, Ricardo. I forgive my father figures — Rick, George, and José. Now, please forgive me for getting Stacey pregnant and not following your order to wait until the marriage. I will serve you for the rest of my life if you allow me to start over with Stacey and our child. I do not want to be a deadbeat dad, a failed father, a fake dad, or a double-standard dad. Please show me how to live a good and Godly life. I dedicate my life to you, Lord God, to Stacey and our child, Amen!

I wasn't "churched." I wasn't a Bible reader. (I was a horrible reader anyway.) I had just started going to church with Stacey and her family. I didn't know how to do this. But I felt like I was finally unshackled and beginning to understand the root of my emotional pain. I could face the pain and pursue healing, or I could reshackle myself by ignoring what I felt and running away.

I started to dream about my childhood goal of playing college football. I reflected on what Jerry and Fran explained to me: they and Stacey still held the high goal of Stacey graduating from North High School and Evangel University. Having a child didn't take those goals away—it just meant more work and greater maturity.

I began to think about our child. What sport would he like? What would she love in life? Would Stacey vote for the name Raúl?

3

BREAKING THE CHAINS

Once I decided not to run away from the emotional pain and not to infect my child with the same psychological injury of not being wanted by his biological father, I embarked on a climb toward greatness: to earn a full-ride scholarship to play collegiate football!

I am not saying that I thought I was great or that I wanted to be the greatest of all time. Rather, I suddenly realized that I had literally been coasting. I was coasting as a student, as an athlete, and with the idea that something would work out for me—or it wouldn't. I wasn't attacking any goal. Thus, my idea of greatness was to leave my mark on North High School. To become greater than I was then—as I stood and looked in the mirror—I knew I had something greater in me. Being 16, without a father or a mentor, my first thought was to go pro in football, the NFL. Man, oh man, would that make my son proud of his dad!

At that time, I was totally focused on outcomes. Being great meant being undefeated! But I began to realize that true greatness was in our pre-season efforts: that was what made me great—or at least led to great outcomes.

But first, I thought I'd better earn a full-ride scholarship to play in college. I needed a full-ride scholarship to afford college. I wanted to improve my reading ability to get accepted into college. I wanted to earn more cash to help with our baby's needs. I wanted to get bigger, faster, and stronger for football.

In the fall of 1986, our sophomore football team went 10–0, the first-ever undefeated sophomore football team in North High history! After the season, our team created a saying: "Going to State in '88. No more beer, no more wine, we are the class of '89!" We started the offseason with most of the guys lifting every morning. However, with basketball and wrestling seasons, the 6 a.m. lifting group steadily dwindled.

I weighed 155 lbs. during the basketball season of my sophomore year. Stacey became pregnant in the spring of our sophomore year, 1987. When we set our goals to get to college, co-parent our child, and (for me) never abandon my child, one of my personal goals was to gain ten pounds. After achieving that, I set another goal to gain ten more pounds, and so on.

Unfortunately, I, too, had already failed my 6 a.m. lifting promise to the team by only going to lift when I felt like it. During track season, my best friend Jeff and I restarted our lifting routine at 6 a.m. every day of school—okay, most days. I started with some raw eggs (Rocky style) and some rice and beans as my pre-workout because we always had leftovers from my grandmother's Mexican restaurant, Ruth's Cosina!

Jeff, on the other hand, was a grab-and-go man. His breakfast of champions was Pop-Tarts or a box of white powdered donuts. We debated about our own breakfast of champions, but interestingly, we actually tied in the bench press, reaching 285 lbs. on our final high school senior year max-outs.

It turns out our key wasn't our breakfast—it was our IRON partnership! As the Holy Bible says, *"Iron sharpens iron, and one man sharpens another"* (Proverbs 27:17 ESV). We literally talked smack and pushed each other daily, and we still do when we get together. Thank you, Best, for sharpening me. I hope you feel the same.

I also found out that I could read better when I had a strong interest. The stronger the interest, the better it seemed. And pictures do help the process and reduce the boredom. I found the *Bigger Faster*

Stronger magazines (BFS) to be an amazing resource. I learned with pictures, formulas for workouts, nutrition, and inspiration.

I subscribed to *Sports Illustrated* magazine and would read articles, especially about workout habits and anything that I thought was within my reach. I went after what I believed would keep me climbing toward my goals. I began snipping out great players in action photos and taped them to the walls of my room. These made a wallpaper header around the top of my wall, all the way around my room. When working out in my room at night, I would visualize being the athlete in the picture and making that big play. As I did, I was definitely moving the needle closer and closer to my next level of greatness. I wasn't fully aware at the time, but my resilient mindset was growing stronger and becoming an inner part of me. My inner man was growing in maturity and confidence.

BUILDING RESILIENCE THROUGH A STRONG WORK ETHIC

A few people had a major influence on me at this time. My grandma Ruth was definitely an MVP! She was my main inspiration growing up. For those of you familiar with Siouxland, she is Ruth, behind Ruth's Cosina, a very popular restaurant in Sioux City, Iowa, in the 1970s–1990s, located in the Stock Yards building.

She was a very strong and outspoken woman and a leader, and she could outwork anyone I had ever seen, including Mexicans with a green card/work visa working 80 hours per week. Nope, Gram put them to shame! They would always challenge her in cooking, cutting, and prepping, and she remained undefeated! I had worked with her since I was ten years old. When I was 16, she said to me, "Mijo, you are very strong. You are the best worker of all the kids. You have to be even stronger and work even harder now." This was her inspiration for me, knowing we had a child on the way.

I must say that my second favorite leader was my mom, but only because I didn't see her very strong work ethic as a skill as I did with my grandma. I saw it as a pain. I had to babysit too often when she had to hold down two or three jobs. It's very interesting looking back now. My mom was the provider for the household, even when she had a paramour living with us. They all mooched off her very strong skillset in the workforce.

So, at ten years old, I could escape babysitting (where I was a "voluntold" unpaid worker) and go to work with Grandma (and get paid). She had me prepping produce in the kitchen, and I got very good very quickly. She paid me cash, which I spent that day at the arcade and bowling. I worked so hard that she promoted me to sous cook at 14, making me her second-in-command even on the busiest weekends. By 16, I became the executive cook on Sundays, opening the kitchen at 7 a.m., prepping with my sous cook, and running the kitchen from 11 a.m. to 9 p.m. Being the boss, even for a day, felt like a new level of greatness!

After Stacey became pregnant, I took on a lot more hours. It was then that people would say, "You should drop out of school and start your own restaurant to support your girlfriend and the baby that is coming." Others said to stop working and get on the government aid programs so Stacey and I could take care of each other. These folks said we would need all the energy and time we could get. It was very difficult to keep my head down and just keep moving, keep climbing, and keep attacking my own goals.

Then there were the conflicting goals between our families: the single-parent home life of a survival-driven, "work even harder" plan from my mom and grandma versus the spiritual-investment plan of "read your Bible, take time in worship and pray," and stay the course dual-parent advice of Jerry and Fran.

It took me a couple of years to realize that the two plans fit together like PB&J on a roasted tortilla! Let's go! Grandma Ruth, you are one of my MVP leaders, and my children and grandchildren thank you!

THE SLIPPERY SLOPE OF A TRAUMATIC PAST

I didn't call it resilience, but I knew my mind was different. I believed in myself for once. I mean, I always had self-confidence, but only in sports. I jumped into challenges when I knew I could win—or at least be a favorite to win.

I started going for things that I previously would not have had the confidence to go after. After a spring and summer of lifting, working, reading, and goal-setting, I felt different, but didn't realize at the time that my thought patterns were different because my daily habits were different!

During my junior year of football in 1987, I earned split time with a couple of senior running backs for a few games. Then, in our third game of the season, I was promoted to starting running back. It was incredible to see mental goals on paper come to life on the field. I hit my stride with several 100-plus-yard games.

Unfortunately, life still disappoints. I dislocated my left shoulder and lost my starting position in football. As the saying goes, "When it rains, it pours." It surely felt that way. During my recovery, I couldn't work as much to make money. I couldn't lift as much to make gains. I couldn't hunt at all. Yes, I pheasant hunted every Saturday in the fall. I hunted in the morning, with friends or alone, then cooked my catch that day and watched some college football before my second shift at Ruth's Cosina. I am an original "Field to Fork" outdoorsman!

So much for awakening my *Resilient Mind*; I was rather downcast in my mood. My old mindset seeped back into my life. I was rude and short with Stacey. My old thought-life sucked, and old sayings from my abusive father figures came rushing back: "You are good for nothing," "You will never be successful," and "Take your @%% back to Mexico." Yes, it literally can happen that fast. Old thought patterns return because the new ones haven't set deep roots yet, and when the storms come, they uproot the work—but not because of the storm. It is 100% the result of my old daily habits becoming the norm again in my life. My physical injury made me believe that I had to stop doing all my mental and spiritual training, too.

In a verbal argument with Stacey, I was so angry over something insignificant that I punched her windshield and shattered it. I tried to push her away from me again and again. An old behavioral habit was to punch holes in my walls in the basement laundry room out of anger —to express physically what was happening to me emotionally. She, in her sweet but utterly stubborn way, just kept saying the same thing, like a broken record. It was annoying. She had a way of calling it like it is. In her own way, she called me a fair-weather fan. When things were going my way, I was tough, fun, and unbreakable, resilient. But when they weren't, I pouted, blamed everyone else, took no responsibility, took zero ownership for the things that I could still accomplish—still under my control—and ran and hid from the truth.

Man, could I ever tell you I loved and hated her at the same time! Wow, the truth hurts. It cuts deep before it heals. Then, it sets you free. Once we are free, we are free indeed (John 8:32).

But why is it so hard to break away from a discouraged mindset? In one of our moments, we had a fight over the phone. I yelled, "Don't ever talk to me again!" I felt like she was rejecting me with how she was trying to help me get over some hurt from my past. She got in her car and drove to my house. When she got there, she honked the horn. I wouldn't come out because I was so mad. She didn't come in because she was crying. I didn't go out because I was stuck in angry self-protection. She sat out in the car, pregnant, for two hours on a fall November day. Two hours of crying, wondering, waiting, and praying. Yes, she told me later she was praying for me!

What? Who are you, and how did I ever deserve you? During this two-hour time frame, every one of my siblings and my mom took turns knocking on my door, telling me, "Um, Stacey is still sitting in her car waiting for you." And I said the same thing to each of them: "Get out!"

The "mysteries of Heaven" are what the Bible calls spiritual things in and out of Heaven. It is times like these when I have experienced these mysteries. At some point near the end of the two hours, I just started crying. And I kept crying. I didn't know then and still don't have *the* reason why, but something broke in me. I am fully convinced that it was Stacey's prayers bombarding Heaven to release a Holy Covering over me, to do what only the Holy Spirit can do! I felt it, like a deep sadness that left me. It was a heaviness down in my gut that all of a sudden felt lighter, more free. I wasn't angry. I realized this wasn't about me. I was going to be a dad—and this is what continued to pull me up and out of my victim mindset of not having a dad or a mentor to fix it for me. No one was coming for me. No one was fixing this for me. It was up to me to protect my child from the psychological injury of abandonment. This suddenly became my main focus again. I went out to sit in the car with Stacey. We cried and prayed to get through the pains that we both had, and for the pains we added to each other. She is quick to forgive and let go. I was willing to forgive but kept the memory in my back pocket just in case I needed ammo for a future fight.

4

SUMMARY: RENEWING YOUR PERSPECTIVE

You will recall, from the introduction of this book, that Romans 12:2 states, *"And be not conformed to this world: but be ye transformed by the renewing of your mind, that ye may prove what is that good, and acceptable, and perfect, will of God."*

Did you see it? Did you see the paths where we were being pushed to close our eyes and blindly follow the "form of those around us?" We were strongly urged to have an abortion. Then, we were strongly pushed to give our child up for adoption. I was mentally pushed to run, hide, and move away. We were asked to have conversations about who would be appropriate for our child if we chose adoption. There are so many times when we hear something that triggers fear, anger, or sadness, and yet we are expected to stand up under the enormous pressure to make mature adult decisions at 16 years old. However, by the grace of God, our Abba Father, we were able to see a possible path to success—but first, we had to develop our *Renewed Perspective!*

PART 1: RENEWING YOUR PERSPECTIVE

This is how we do it: Renewing your perspective means seeing your thoughts in an objective format so that you can disengage from them as your own. Instead, we must see our thoughts as possibilities connected to both immediate and delayed consequences. Once this is done, we no longer own thoughts; we implement them like pieces of a larger puzzle—a means to an end. We always choose the end—because choosing an action based on a thought is always connected to its consequences. "Action has consequences" is what I teach in our clinic, and most agree that it is true. However, most people disagree with this teaching in my clinic, "Thoughts have consequences," especially if you are conforming to the pattern of thoughts of others. Thus, we are *always choosing our consequences*, either subconsciously via old habits or consciously via objective truths. To control our consequences, we must first be able to control our way of thinking: our renewed thought patterns.

We are often bombarded by external stimuli that hinder our own train of thought. It has been speculated that our brains take in millions of bits of data per second. Our conscious brain is only capable of processing hundreds to thousands, not millions, of bits per second. Our *perspective*—what we actively see, hear, or perceive—processes approximately seven thoughts per second.

From my 25 years of clinical experience, most people can only discuss the thoughts they "pull down." Imagine you are at a red light. You glance up to the left and see the running report moving across a huge LED screen with the daily news, weather, and updates scrolling across the screen. The light turns green, and you drive away. Kids may be talking in the car. The radio is playing music. The only thing you're focused on is the one issue your brain deemed a high enough priority to process: *Wow, a heat index of 107 today? No way, I hope my child's game is canceled. I mean, I want to go, but come on, sitting on a smoking hot aluminum bleacher and sweating through my clothes? No, thank you!*

The point is this: Despite the tens of millions of bits our subconscious brain encodes and the hundreds our conscious mind takes in, we can only process one thought of the handful that scroll across our mind's eye per second. Then, we choose to pull down a thought and open up the concept. This is where one can get triggered, stuck, offended, hurt, angry, flustered, confused, and even lost. The Bible puts it this way:

"... and the peace of God, which surpasses all understanding, will guard your hearts and minds through Christ Jesus." (Philippians 4:7 KJV)

It is a full-time job to guard our hearts and minds from the complete invasion of our subconscious and conscious thoughts. The one thought that gets pulled down from a batch leads to our belief systems, which either act as a catalyst or a fire extinguisher to our daily goals. If we only knew that every thought we allow into our mind's eye is already attached to a consequence—positive or negative—we would truly guard our hearts and minds with more fervor because words are truly life or death (Proverbs 18:21). If not behaviorally, then for sure mentally, emotionally, and spiritually!

Let's revisit some of the major pivots that Stacey and I took in order not to conform to the world—but to Renew Our Perspective. Some of the life-altering statements and thoughts are highlighted below:

Planned Parenthood Center Counselor:
- "We will find more suitable parents."

Fran's perspective:
- "The Holy Spirit told me."
- "I will stay home so you both can stay in school."

Jerry's perspective:
- "Your life isn't ruined, it's just different."

Linda's perspective:
- "You will have to drop out of school and work hard to cover it all."

My perspective:
- "I need to move to Texas."
- "I am not good enough for Stacey."
- "I am not wanted."
- "I am too broken to be saved."
- "Yes, I believe in God, but I am not sure about Jesus."
- "I will not infect my child with the same pain of not having a dad."

Stacey's perspective:
- "My life is ruined."
- "The Planned Parenthood counselor made me feel worthless."
- "No, I am not giving up my baby for adoption."
- "I love you."
- "Jesus loves you because He died for you."
- "Yes, I would still be in love with you if I weren't pregnant."
- "You are enough for me."
- "I cannot promise that I will not disappoint you, but I will never leave you."
- "I cannot help you feel wanted if you keep kicking me out."
- "We are in this together; you are stuck with me—forever!"
- "No, my parents don't hate you."
- "No, my sisters don't hate you."
- "It's not too late; Jesus already died for you."

"I can do all things through Christ which strengthens me"
(Philippians 4:13 KJV)

So, how do we move from our own mental prison to our Renewed Perspective that sets us on our path to mental and spiritual freedom?

The key to Renewing Your Perspective is in your self-talk. Look at how Stacey responded to me. Her tendencies were to knock down my emotional pains and insecurities from being abandoned by my birth dad and being left out by my stepdad and other figures. Based on how she responded, you can get very close to guessing my questions and my detrimental, hurtful self-talk. If you haven't discovered it yet,

Stacey had a more *Resilient Mind* than I did, and she mentored me in this direction to a new level of greatness!

All glory to God the Father, YAHWEH, that I was able to be vulnerable with Stacey; otherwise, I would have kept running from the emotional pain and kept myself locked in my own mental prison. Her ability to just sit and speak her truth, to be authentically herself and share scriptures, to be still, quiet, and pray—these were the keys. She would often put on a Christian song to change the atmosphere, helping me change my mindset, which had me chained to the pains and mistakes of my past.

To this day, when someone calls Stacey to share a private prayer request about their family situation, one of the very first things she says is: "Turn on KLOVE or a Christian playlist and allow the God of the Universe to broadcast His presence and His authority into the atmosphere of your home." Yes, this is what she started with me when we were a couple of 16-year-olds facing the greatest opportunity of our lives!

I had to accept what Stacey was sharing with me. Then I started to believe it for myself. The behavioral work followed—reading, praying, and singing praises to Yahweh.

I had to believe what the Bible was saying about me. The hard part wasn't believing her and the Bible; it was learning to shed the harsh emotional pains that had been routinely spoken over me and my life by my failing father figures—repeated continuously over the first 14 years of my life. Shedding those would be shedding my chains of bondage! Easier said than done, I agree. Easier now than tomorrow. It gets easier over repeated trials. The repeated trials create new patterns of thinking, new behaviors, then new habits, and a new cycle of life for your generational living legacy!

In the present day, 2024, I live to lead people to the pathway of freedom from their mental prison. Their mental prison makes you believe that the storm ruined your life. The mental prison feels as if everyone knows the broken links in your armor, and thus, nobody can help you, nor will they ever want to.

In reality, it only made them *believe* they had to stop their new daily habits that were causing neuroplasticity in the mind—new pathways and new bundles of neurons that fire together and rewire together. When the new habits halt, so do the new thought patterns…and our default mode (subconscious programming developed over years of trials) kicks back into gear to run the show. This is why I love to use my "Living Legacy Coaching programs" to reach the masses and set the captives free from their own mental prison!

"There's

**To Be Great: When You Feel Like It
And When You Don't!"**™

PART II

MOVING TOWARD UNCERTAINTY

(I) And be not conformed to this world,
(II) but be ye transformed by the renewing of your mind,
(III) that ye may prove what is that good, and acceptable, and perfect, will of God. (Romans 12:2, KJV)

ACTION STEP II: MOVE TOWARD UNCERTAINTY!

"Life is like riding a bicycle, to keep your balance, you must keep moving."
– Albert Einstein

5

RESILIENCE

Webster's Dictionary defines **resilience** (noun) as the capability of a strained body to recover its size and shape after deformation caused especially by compressive stress. An ability to recover from or adjust easily to misfortune or change.

The word resilience derives from the present participle of the Latin verb *resiliere*, meaning "to jump back" or "to recoil." The base of *resiliere* is *salire*, a verb meaning "to leap" that also pops up in the etymologies of such sprightly words as sally and somersault.

My definition of resilience includes a concept best illustrated with an image. Picture a small rubber ball (a Super Ball) known for its extreme bounce. It's the kind you buy for a quarter, and when you turn the silver wheel of the gumball machine, the neon-colored ball drops into your hand.

Now, imagine that you are a Super Ball, and each time you fall and hit the ground, you rebound, recovering the size, shape, and energy initially lost. We would say, "You are resilient," in line with the definition provided above.

Next, I want you to imagine that every time you hit the ground (take a fall, get pushed down, hit a wall, experience a failure, or experience a traumatic event), if you can rebound/recover, then you actually grow. But what do you grow? This is where my definition of resilience differs from the rest, to add the emotional growth that is protective against the next fall.

I want you to imagine that you are trying to do something new, let's say, play pickleball. This is your very first time, and your young adult son is teaching you the basics.

With each new *attempt* to swing at the ball, to serve the ball, to dink the ball, you feel like it's getting worse—like, no, really, "I am starting to stink the place up with my terrible play."

As our expectations grow and the learning curve gets steeper, your son continues to add to his technique. This can bring a feeling of heaviness and some forms of emotional pain, like embarrassment—the intersection of reality versus desire—and the ever-present notion that "I have a long way to go."

What if I told you that you are literally building resiliency? With each new serve, swing, and dink, you are growing through the number of *successive attempts*, and that's what makes you more and more resilient.

It's not about successful *attempts* initially; it's about the number of *successive attempts*. The more you *attempt*, the more you grow—and the more quickly you engage in *successive attempts*, the more quickly you grow.

TRY VERSUS ATTEMPT

It is common to think of a "try" as being equal to an *"attempt."* I have always been a fan of Yoda; he said it best in *The Empire Strikes Back*, **"Do. Or do not. There is no try."**

I work with a lot of people who have very restricted food preferences, often called the *Few-Foods Diet* as it relates to ADHD (Attention-Deficit/Hyperac-tivity Disorder), and they all strongly believe in the word "try." It often goes like this: "Yes, I tried it. I smelled it, then touched it to my lips, and I knew I didn't like it." This is a great example of a "try." It's like a one-and-done type approach to say, without actually saying, "I don't want to."

For the purpose of building resilience, we do not believe in a "try." Instead, we engage in the teaching of effortful "attempts." In the example above, an *attempt* would involve cutting a bite-sized piece of food, dividing it into two micro pieces, and then making effortful attempts to eat each one until the bite-sized portion is consumed. This process allows for an informed decision to be made.

According to AskDifference.com, the main distinction between "try" and "attempt" is that *try* implies engaging in an action without much regard for the outcome. It's often said that people *try* something simply to say, "Well, I tried." In contrast, an *attempt* reflects intentional effort aimed at achieving a specific goal. An *attempt* is often used to show progress toward completing a difficult or official task. In short, *try* is typically associated with a one-time effort—such as "I tried that soup"—whereas *attempt* implies ongoing effort until a goal is reached.

Failure (missed attempts) makes most people shy away from continued participation. The number one reason people stop any new activity (pickleball, tennis, running, healthy diet, losing weight, gaining muscle, writing a book, etc.) is that "I wasn't seeing any progress." The reverse is also true. The number one reason people stick with a new activity is because "the results came quickly."

So, how do we grow resiliency to grow results quickly? Resilience is built with each new effortful attempt at building consistency of repetitions. This is like earning one new rubber band wrapped tightly around a Super Ball. Every new attempt earns us a new rubber band. The rubber bands become our *resiliency bands* that buffer us from stress, failure, and quitting.

Resilience, therefore, actively and speedily grows the number of rubber bands. This is how we at Renewing The Mind define and build resiliency—*by stacking the resiliency bands as fast as possible!*

The rubber bands never guarantee success. The rubber bands always guarantee more immunity to failure—an inoculation against quitting; a bumper of resiliency. The bigger the bumper, the greater the level of resiliency!

Your mindset is no longer about achieving rapid gains/outcomes. Instead, your mindset is locked in on growing the number of successive attempts. This new experience of gaining immunity from the feeling of failure no longer limits your number of attempts. Your training sessions now only stop when you have hit the number of successive attempts you set as your goal prior to your training.

Of course, your goal continues to be to hit a successful serve, forehand, dink—but I am only counting successive attempts, as this is my immunity to failure. Yes, successful attempts still earn a rubber band—they are still attempts! Yes, successful attempts grow confidence much faster by increasing the size of your immunity: the number of resiliency bands.

Finally, imagine a person with five attempts earning five rubber bands and another with 250 attempts earning 250 rubber bands. Even if we say that both the five and the 250 are only failures—attempts that did not hit the mark—they are still effortful attempts nonetheless.

The person with more attempts still has more immunity against failure, against getting stuck in their head, against giving up on their dream life, against quitting on themselves.

Why is this the case? It happens because the Super Ball that has 250 rubber bands has a very thick bumper—thick skin—that protects against giving up: an immunity to excuses. The Super Ball with five rubber bands has a very small bumper that isn't a strong immune system against excuses and quitting.

Imagine the difference between a person attempting something anxiety-provoking, like public speaking at their home church. It's definitely anxiety-provoking because public speaking is the number one universal fear. It's also a semi-warm audience, as some people in the crowd may be family and friends. Finally, imagine a person with zero attempts on stage versus a person with 50 on-stage speaking attempts. The issue is never about success and failure (outcomes); rather, it is only about the resiliency earned with each new attempt.

An experimental example of the power of resiliency when facing fear or experiencing a failed attempt is shown below.

Allow me to introduce to you a beginner Super Ball (Figure 1) and a resilient Super Ball (Figure 2).

Resilient Mind

Figure 1: *Beginner super ball with zero attempts/resilience bands*

The beginner Super Ball has never attempted a new activity that is anxiety-provoking. Either he refuses to attempt because it is too scary (trying a new piece of seafood, etc), or he cannot see that the attempt actually helps him grow. He sees only a failed attempt in his mind. Thus, his self-talk leads him to avoid an attempt because he cannot mentally carry that thought of failing.

Figure 2: *Intermediate super ball with 50 new attempts/resilience bands*

The intermediate Super Ball represents a person who has learned to move into the uncertainty of making new and repeated attempts at an anxiety-provoking activity. She is aware of the possibility of a failed attempt, and she has learned to count any new attempts as successive approximations of earning the skill. She knows that making more attempts means getting closer and closer to perfecting her new skill. Thus, her self-talk moves her into uncertainty because she cannot hold the thought of never attempting and being stuck in the same position a month from today.

Perhaps you are wondering why the intermediate mindset no longer dwells on the question, "What if I fail?" This is precisely the essence of resiliency: repeated attempts at any new task or skill build layers of resilience, which, over time, develop a very thick skin. This thick skin (bands of resilience) is literally an inoculation from *Fear, Uncertainty, Doubt,* and *Shame* (FUDS) because she is stuck in the "one more rep," or "let's run it back," or "I haven't hit 10 in a row yet." This inoculation is what we call a *Resilient Mind*! Yes, fear, uncertainty, doubt, and shame will come–especially in the face of a new big opportunity–it's normal. However, the FUDS do not penetrate her mind because her bands of resilience protect her, buffer her, and allow her to keep moving into the FUDS as her eyes are on the prize…"One more rep!" This is the secret sauce to a *Resilient Mind*!

Interestingly, we all inherently know this phenomenon. Almost everyone who hears this process states, "It makes sense." I do not recall anyone stating, "Nope, that's impossible," "I can't believe it," or "This blew my mind." It is a simple concept that we all inherently know.

When we only attempt something a few times, we often self-protect by saying, "Well, if I practiced (attempted) as much as you, I would be great too!" It's true, admit it—you are guilty. I am guilty of this statement in golf, pickleball, writing, and more!

When studying and then earning a lower grade than a peer, I would often say, "Well, I only glanced at my notes, and I'm sure you spent hours studying." Perhaps this is true in a lot of areas of your life, too. Take a deep breath, a long exhale, and focus on your past for a moment. It's there, isn't it? It's okay; we are all in this together. We either get to play dumb and stay stuck in the cycles of fear, or we get to learn and grow increasingly more *resilient* by adding more and more successive attempts!

FAILING FAST

We have taught each of our children to ride a bike without training wheels in one day, usually within an hour. This is how we did it. Allow me to demonstrate to you the difference between trying and attempting in regards to learning to ride a bike without training wheels.

Example one. Parent and child embark on a journey to learn how to ride a bike. Parent runs behind the child and holds onto the bike seat. All is well until the child gets anxious and overcorrects the handlebars and wipes out. They go inside, clean up the scrape on the knee, and administer a Band-Aid. The child is too afraid to make another try; therefore, they decide to give it a break for today. The parent tries to encourage the child to try again the next day, but the fears are too great, so they don't try again until one week later. Unfortunately, it results in the exact same activity and the exact same result.

Example number two. Parent runs behind the child to hold onto the bike seat. All is well until the child gets anxious, overcorrects the handlebars, and wipes out. They go inside, clean up the scrape on the knee, and administer a Band-Aid. This time, however, they incentivize the child with extra privileges to make another attempt. On their second attempt, a few minutes later, the parent notices that when the child overcorrects, they continue to countersteer, so the child does not wipe out but recovers. They then make a third attempt and ride for the same amount of time, have a near miss, and wipe out again. They make a fourth attempt and ride a little bit longer. On the fifth attempt, after the child oversteers and wipes out, the parent brushes off the dust and talks about all of the success the child is having and how fast and far she has been riding. She begins to smile; she's no longer anxious, and now has a little bit of fun and excitement and knows that she can do this. They embark on attempt number six, and she rides almost the whole block with a huge smile. The joy of reaching a goal and experiencing the fun, the excitement, and the freedom is now her "why to let it fly!"

You might be asking yourself, *So it's all based on incentivizing a child?* No, the incentive just helped to get the child's eyes off of the fear, uncertainty, doubt, or shame. The real secret sauce in this process is *failing fast.*

With each new overcorrection or near wipeout, the parent continues to push forward on the bike by running behind her as she learns to pedal *through* the struggle and not panic and dump the bike. Her bands of resilience are stacking as fast as possible.

The active ingredient inside the secret sauce is her *joy*. When she first overcorrected and wiped out, everything centered upon the fear and uncertainty of getting back on the bike. The only way to combat this is *through* it. Once she began to experience the joy and the freedom of pedaling her bike, especially faster than her dad, there was nothing to hold her back.

Let's take a look at the data from the first day we trained our daughter on how to ride a bike without training wheels. In example one, the child finished day one with one band of resilience wrapped around her as a form of inoculation from fear, uncertainty, doubt, and shame. She also associates the bike with pain and injury, as that was her only experience.

In contrast, the child, in example two, finished day one of training with 12 bands of resilience wrapped around her, which is a good start to her immunity to fear, uncertainty, doubt, and shame. She now also associates the bike with fun and a feeling of pure joy from the independence of the wind on her face! *This is building resiliency, one band of resilience per effortful attempt, by failing fast!*

In our Renewing The Mind Podcast (www.youtube.com/renewingthemindpodcast), we state: "*You don't know what you don't know, but once you know, you can never unknow.*" So now you know! No more excuses, only more successive *attempts*!

6

ATTEMPTING RESILIENCY

After the reality hit that we were going to be parents, I made a decision to grow in all areas. A lot changed between the spring of 1987 and December 28, 1987. I was learning that resiliency is indeed developed through successive repetition—through *attempts*.

I started reading my Bible while lying in bed before going to sleep. All I had was a King James Version (KJV), and that form of language is difficult to read—especially for a dyslexic, "Spanglish"-speaking teen.

I began with the beginning: Genesis 1:1-4:

1. "In the beginning, God created the heavens and the earth.
2. And the earth was without form and void, and darkness was upon the face of the deep. And the Spirit of God moved upon the face of the waters.
3. And God said, Let there be light: and there was light.
4. And God saw the light, that it was good: and God divided the light from the darkness."

This was a rather difficult time for me. I would read, then read it again, and when still frustrated, I would take a break and come back to it. I often became frustrated and quit. I would ask Stacey, and if she didn't understand either, she would ask her parents, and they would help with the literal meaning and the spiritual implication of the Holy scriptures—The Word of Yahweh.

In my pain and frustration, I began reading the Bible to prove it wrong. Perhaps it was jealousy of how Stacey was raised versus my life: I was reading to find proof that the Fish family wasn't perfect.

I wish it wasn't true, but I was reading the Bible to prove to myself that "Christians are not perfect." People who know this piece of our story have asked, "Why were you out to get Christians?" The truth is that I wasn't. It was out of my pure frustration/jealousy that Stacey and her parents, Jerry and Fran Fish, seemed to have it all together. They were the closest thing to the Cleavers from the hit TV sitcom *Leave It to Beaver* that I had ever seen in my young life, and it was a little creepy for me.

No, I wasn't out to get them.

No, I wasn't angry at them.

No, it isn't possible to be that happy that often.

No, I did not deserve them.

No, I definitely did not deserve Stacey!

Yes, it seemed too good to be true.

Yes, Stacey told her parents everything, and I felt violated, exposed, and misunderstood.

Yes, I felt like they were getting too close to me.

Yes, I was feeling more and more vulnerable: I had never let a girlfriend in before.

Yes, I felt like once they understood my past—the truth of the trauma—they would just leave me, abandon me, and reinforce what I already knew—I wasn't good enough for them. I didn't know it then, but I had a very strong fear of rejection and abandonment. I discovered this in my training at NDSU and the University of Iowa. It was crazy because I didn't know when it turned on or off. It was like the flip of a light switch: all or nothing, no dimmer adjustments whatsoever.

"What is this light switch?" you ask. It is none other than my *self-protection* skillset. It's on, or it's off. And I didn't have the remote control. I would subconsciously undermine what Stacey and her parents were trying to do, which was to disciple me in *The Way* of Jesus

Christ. They wanted to show me that yes—"For all have sinned, and come short of the glory of God." (Romans 3:23). And yet, "For whosoever shall call upon the name of the Lord shall be saved." (Romans 10:13).

Interestingly, I do not ever recall them teaching to me, preaching to me, or ever confronting me about anything. Instead, I always felt welcome, seen, heard, and as if they were genuinely interested in me as a person. Each time I visited, they always wanted a report of my sports, family, and pursuits, and they reminded me that "we are praying for you!"

What?! Who does that? Wow, I mean, you are praying for me? Thanks! I know I didn't do anything to deserve you, Stacey, or your prayers, and I'll take it!

Wait, what? Are you trying to find dirt on me? Are you trying to deport me? Well, the joke's on you, John Wayne; I was born in Texas! You know the saying, "Don't Mess with Texas!" Then, out of nowhere, I would get emotionally hurt; I felt like I was on stage and I was being mocked. All my fear statements listed above would play on repeat.

So, I would get really quiet as I tried to work through my silent anger—my *self-protection*. I wanted to leave, but Stacey wanted more time with me, so we would retreat to a TV room and talk. She knew something was wrong, and I didn't want to tell her. But I couldn't, even if I wanted to, as I was blind to my own "silent anger." What if I told you it wasn't truly anger? It was a subconscious engine that turns on when it detects harm, overexposure, or incongruence. For me, my silent treatment wasn't anger but more of an inner brooding, and this process fuels the energy to walk away from something you love—but it's better to be safe than sorry, right? The engine is called fear.

The fear of rejection.

The fear of abandonment.

The fear of not being good enough.

The fear of being exposed as a fake or imposter.

The fear that when Stacey sees behind the curtain, she will surely leave me!

It felt like I had a fake ID and got instant access—"I am in like Flynn!" Then that sinking feeling of one of these times when they call my name and I acknowledge the request to engage in more conversation, but this time they ID me for real, and they escort me to the door and kick me out—forever!

PEPPERDINE UNIVERSITY

My first meeting and impression of Jerry Fish was an example of living with a fake ID. After I asked Stacey to go to homecoming, we began hanging out. One day, she invited me over to her house. I was so nervous. I searched for an outfit that would be both impressive and subtle. I found my friend Jeff's Pepperdine University sweatshirt that I had snagged from his house. I put on some nice jeans and penny loafers. Yes, I was a jock, but it felt right to dress like a prep for that seemingly special occasion. I didn't know if we would hang out with her parents or just the two of us, so I wanted to make a great first impression.

Jerry answered the door. I didn't know it then, but we all laugh about it now: Jerry is like a walking encyclopedia, so no matter what the topic is, he's ready and willing to elaborate on everything.

What I had hoped would be a simple handshake and introduction turned into an interview about why I should consider Pepperdine University Law School. After all, they are world-renowned, and the marketability of a law degree from such a prestigious university would be a golden ticket across the country. He went on to discuss the benefits of being bilingual and doubling the reach of my law degree. This way, we could have two law offices in one—English-speaking clients and Spanish-speaking clients.

I mean, perhaps I'm at fault as well, as I didn't have the courage to tell him I snagged the sweatshirt from my friend Jeff, and it actually belonged to Jeff's oldest sister, Janet. He was so inspired, and I was so lost. I must have seemed convincing enough to carry the conversation by saying "yes" and "no" at the right times because it just kept going and going.

I didn't even know where Pepperdine was located. Thankfully, he mentioned the amazing California campus, so I had something to run with; otherwise, he would have known I was a fake.

I was so thankful for Fran. She must have overheard the conversation because she came and got me, escorting me to the TV room where we hung out together. This is when I was introduced to Georgia-style sweet tea! It was the best tea I had ever tasted, and it changed my life.

Stacey, Fran, and I hung out, watching Friday night sitcoms and just talking. It was fun and relaxing, and somehow, I felt like I belonged. Fran had the sweetest personality; she was so warm and seemingly accepting. We talked a bit about my love for Michigan Wolverine football, and she was born and raised in Ohio—enough said about that JV team from the South. It was so easy, so peaceful, and so welcoming. I had already chased down Stacey, and now I was feeling like maybe I was welcome; maybe I fit in here, even if I had to run with a lie to fit in.

RESILIENCE ISN'T GIVEN

The very odd thing was that this *engine of fear* was losing its grip on my behavior, or at least I was becoming more aware of it. Yes, it was still there and still influential in my life. However, I was able to test my thoughts, not in the moment, but after some workout time at home, I was able to reflect.

It went something like this...

They are trying to trap me somehow. They are "too nice too often" because they are just trying to convert me to Christianity. They only care about growing their own church. Maybe they want me to get better so I can be better with Stacey and our child. They want me to be better because Stacey loves me—or maybe she is only staying with me because she is pregnant?

This would often send me into an angry mood and that *self-protection* response that was like a knee-jerk reaction to stress, fear, and rejection. I wasn't able to talk about it because it was embedded anger and fear, and it all came out as a form of pressure. I was, praise the Lord, able to release the pressure from workouts—weights, running, biking, and jumping rope.

Hours after my workout, I was able to pull up my list. I don't forget much, and I was a pro at holding onto grudges. This "burn list" of how often someone has burned me before was the only thing I used to help me know who can be trusted—but I did not have anything on Stacey.

She never burned me... yet. If she did, she apologized as soon as she recognized she did something that could be interpreted that way. Initially, all I had against her was the suspicion that she could be faking it all just to keep me with her instead of being another pregnant teen with no partner.

Therefore, I would always resettle on the notion that she was for me, not against me, that she had never hurt me, that she always apologized as soon as possible, and that she always wanted more time with me—but why?

This was a turning point for me. This process of testing my thoughts and testing my offenses by checking my "burn list" allowed me to continue gaining more and more attempts at:

- Knocking down my wall
- Knocking down my self-protective cues
- Knocking down my judgmental thoughts of Stacey, Jerry, and Fran
- Knocking down my fear of rejection, abandonment, and feeling mocked
- Building my trust with Stacey
- Building my trust in our relationship
- Building my trust in the Bible
- Building my trust in myself
- Building my trust in my ability to develop into a good dad!

It's so crazy to look back and see all the pitfalls that could have swallowed me up for very little offense. I mean, I was so emotionally sensitive that I would opt out of things that were difficult for me instead of building any resiliency. However, in areas where I had already built some resiliency, I was almost unbeatable—like in sports, workouts, and pushing myself for more, where I had established small sustainable steps toward more attempts.

If you had told me that I was emotionally sensitive, emotionally weak, or fragile, I would have probably beat you up. My self-protection was so strong that I was ready to defend my position without any questioning. It was swing first; test the burn list later. Thankfully, after being on probation and working with my probation officer (P.O.), I learned to complete as much work as possible today rather than putting it off until tomorrow. I finished all my community service hours and P.O. sessions in six months instead of a year. I then applied this new skillset to my workouts. I was learning to work out today to release any anger and pain rather than holding onto it to see if it would just go away on its own. It was a game-changer for my life. It was a perfect fit for me because I used to take long bike rides to escape the abuse from my stepdad, so it felt natural for me to work out to reduce my anger, pain, and fear.

This is where I locked down my successive attempts in workouts—the process of failing fast—by stacking rubber bands of resilience.

Initially, I only worked out to cool down, process my anger, release my fear, and convince myself that I didn't need anyone. Later on, workouts became a safe place for me to see myself—the good, the bad, and the ugly. I am safe. I am enough. I am strong. I am resilient!

7

CHRISTMAS WITH TYLER

It happened during the Christmas break of our junior year of high school. Tyler Curtis Sánchez was born on December 28, 1987. There were 9 lbs. and one oz. of him. I wholeheartedly believe the hand of God was in it, all the way back to when her parents found out, and I cried out to Jesus.

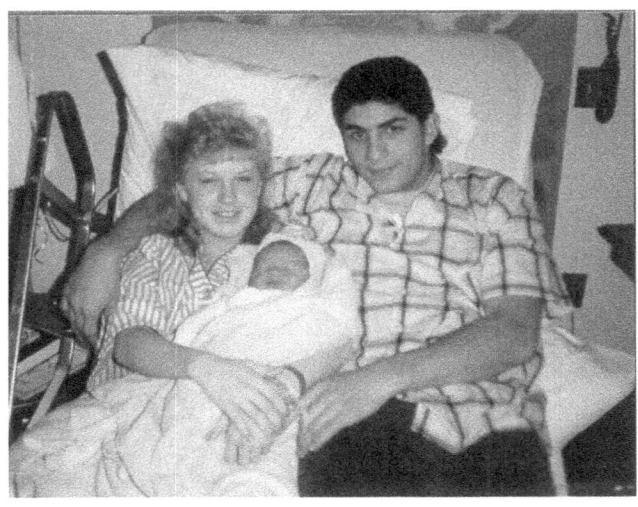

(Stacey (16), Raúl (17), newborn baby Tyler at the hospital)

My mental eyes were opened. I saw things differently. People who had abused and wrecked me never broke me. I used to write down *"I WILL NOT BE BROKEN"* all over my room to remind me that "although you abused me, you will never break me." I still have *"I WILL NOT BE BROKEN"* as the title of my 5 a.m. alarm! But I was starting to realize that those encounters (abuse) also educated me. Having a son was just the thing I needed to get out of my own way.

Since it was over Christmas break, we had so many visitors. Being in high school meant a lot of friends. When they all would congregate in our room and hang out with us, we would often get scolded by a Nurse Ratched-type (from the movie *One Flew Over the Cuckoo's Nest*) who did not take kindly to us being over our four-visitor limit.

(Our hospital room is full of Stacey's friends)

Tyler's last name was Fish. I had overheard a conversation between Stacey and Fran. They were talking about how having a child with a different last name as a single mother would not be a good thing for Stacey. In other words, if that boy, Raúl, didn't stick around, it wouldn't be good for another man in the future to see her son have a different last name than Stacey.

The old me would have bolted away from the shame and anger in order to hide from this type of pain: discrimination of something I couldn't fix, my brown skin, and different ethnicity. The old me would have looked for someone, a female friend, to help me ignore the pain of rejection altogether. I quickly realized that anger and emotional pain place a lid on the truth.

Working through the anger and pain allowed me to find and understand the truth, even if it was ugly. This was *their* truth for Stacey. If I wasn't around, Stacey and her child would have the same last name. It was their solution; it was their plan B.

My truth was, *I'm not going anywhere!* Nor did I want to. When I think about this time in my life, I can still feel the energy that allowed me to stay and fight for my child.

Initially, Stacey and I argued over it. I chose to take offense at what Fran said. Stacey was able to calm me down by reminding me of who her mom really was with her loving heart. She meant well, although it sounded like she was against me. She was actually doing better than me, putting Tyler's protection and interests first, ahead of my own feelings.

I became okay with Tyler's last name being Fish. I wasn't fighting to hide from emotional pain anymore. I was rolling with things and interpreting only what I needed in order to level up in my personal goals. I was getting rid of things I could not control and focusing more and more on what I could be responsible for and to see how quickly I could level up.

We decided Tyler was going to live with Stacey and Fran on weekdays. My mom worked full time. Fran could stay home. I was going to take Tyler every weekend, on Friday, after sports practice through Sunday night.

The crib in my bedroom was a nice touch, set apart from the aggressive athlete side of me. It allowed me to keep my eyes on the prize. Even when Tyler was at Stacey's house, I used that crib as visual motivation to never go back, to never accept the default mindset—set upon fear of failing—that I once thought was my own mind.

I started not to believe in what others said about me. Think of all the junk that an unguarded mind can accumulate on its own. Then, imagine what gets attracted to a mind that feels unwanted by the suicide of a biological father. Add what three other broken men had dropped on me, with addictions, physical abuse of me, and domestic abuse of my mom. Think of the mentality of any father figure already battling their own addictions, demons, and past traumas. Just as my biological father isn't who I am, I was not any of my stepfathers.

When I saw my son's crib late at night, it sometimes made me cry. I would relive old emotional pains, incidents of serious physical abuse, or the emotional pain of seeing when my mom was being beaten up. Then, I would work out with my dumbbells and jump rope to identify and push through the emotional pain. As I worked out, I would pray, "Lord, if it is in your will to let me parent Tyler his whole life, I promise you that I will never leave him or forsake him just as you have promised it to me!"

> "Keep your life free from the love of money, and be content with what you have, for he has said, 'I will never leave you nor forsake you.'"
> (Hebrews 13:5 ESV)

It is crazy to think about those days and look back at them, but that crib was an altar for me. I could look at Tyler's crib and see the hand of God. He was taking our sin, sex before marriage, and making it into an altar of prayer and rebirth for me. I realize this may sound like blasphemy or a bad romance novel. But I promise you that the emotional, mental, and spiritual work was just beginning to develop resilience and renew my mind.

People who know our story often ask, "How did you start believing in God, Jesus, and the Bible so quickly?" I didn't feel like it was so fast. It was over our two-year courtship, while Stacy was pregnant, knowing a child was coming, becoming a parent, and the desperate desire never to be my dad or any of my other father figures to my child. This process lit a fear in me to chase God and truly test it for me. What actually ended up happening was that I truly started to test Jesus as my father. Thus, my answer is this: "I was naive enough to believe Jesus is my dad."

The amazing thing for me was that I was becoming aware of what was *truly me* and what was only fronting as me, like a skin in a video game that was hiding who I truly was. It is incredible to know that God can make an impulsive choice to make provision for sin, resulting in significant stress and fear (I was a 17-year-old father), and allow it to be a turning point of healing, of resilience, and of renewal.

8

RESILIENCY HAS FEET

As I began to walk out my developing *Resilient Mindset* by doing the work I said I would do, I continued to hit that wall of *This is not how I saw it in my mind.* Doubt set in, and it seemed easier to just let go of the stress, strain, and goals. It felt as if I was walking uphill in every direction. Nothing seemed easy. Everything seemed designed to oppose me and each one of my goals. I still had a temper. It was easy to control when things were going my way, but the old mindset showed its ugly head far too often.

Following my junior year of football—my comeback season—I decided not to go out for basketball so I could get bigger, faster, stronger, and make more money for our child's expenses. I was well-prepared for baseball and track season.

My baseball season was rough, however, as opponents from other teams had heard about me becoming a father. They yelled profanities at me when I was at bat, made a play, or ran the bases.

Once, I was angry at a shortstop and a third baseman as they continued to harass me the entire game. While attempting to steal third base, the ball and the tag had me beat. Out of anger, during my slide, I lifted my leg and kicked the third baseman with my cleats, knocking him off the bag and onto his back. It was obvious to the umpire that it was a retaliation. I was thrown out of the game. This anger episode made me realize I wasn't as far along in my resiliency as I had hoped. I realized I needed to push harder, achieve more, and climb above the noise and the haters. It never broke me, but it was a constant reminder that the haters would never go away—and neither would being a father. Being a father is forever.

As part of this new push, I began asking coaches questions about college and asking players about their plans. I discovered several people had already taken a test called the ACT to get into college. Some told me about an ACT study book that I could check out and use to prepare for the big test. I spoke with my baseball coach, Bud Speraw, who was also my high school academic advisor. He told me to sign up for a time to talk to him about college. So, I signed up.

When I went in to talk to him, he had my academic file on his desk. I explained that I was getting some offers to play college football and needed to know what to do next. He explained that those letters were probably not "promissory" but simply inquiries to gauge my level of interest in applying or not.

So, I was not being recruited as an athlete? Coach Speraw said, "Most definitely not."

Whoa, bro, slow your roll, my dude! We were undefeated as sophomores, and this year, I was a starting running back. I dislocated my shoulder, came back, and won the starting job back again. I was one of the stars on both these teams. I was definitely getting letters!

The coach didn't seem to care. He continued to pore over my academic file.

Silence.

More silence.

Then he sat back in his office chair, threw his hands behind his head, and clasped his fingers together behind his neck. His elbows were wide, and his chest was puffed out. He exhaled and said, "Kid, you are just not college material."

This was a huge rejection. I did not do well with rejection. As Coach started talking about trade school and a local community college, I interrupted and said, "You don't even know me, so how can you say this?"

He repeated his statement, "Kid, you are just not college material."

I slammed my hand on the desk. I was getting emotionally charged; my resiliency was slipping through my fingers. "My goal isn't to go to college just to party! It's to play college football on a scholarship so I can focus on my studies and not spend all my time on a part-time job."

Coach returned his hands to his desk and flipped the folder open. He spun the reports so that they faced me. "I have a saying: 'If you know it, then you will show it.' And kid, you just don't show it!"

As I began to argue a third time, he pointed to one of my school reports. He told me I should be high on the percentile breakdown for various subjects. Most kids that went to college were well above a certain line. I had reached the line only once in science. As I looked at my scores, I said, "Do you mean those stupid Iowa Tests of Basic Skills (ITBS) we take in the library? Dude, I don't even try at all. I get bored, and I just do a dot-to-dot with them because I don't even know why we take them or what they are used for."

He just said, "If you know it, you will show it, and you just don't show it." He continued, "You are a very hard worker and have a lot of other skills…"

I slammed my hand on the desk again and yelled, "I am going to college! Watch me!"

When I tell this story to kids at an assembly or a conference, the most common thing they say is, "Man, your guidance counselor was a jerk!"

But that interview with my coach was a major turning point for me. To this day, I can vividly see him and hear his voice. I have replayed that conversation in my memory over and over and over again—forever! It did nothing to break me or deter me. Instead, it was the greatest spark of deep determination for me academically. And that academic determination sparked a more athletic drive to prove I was being recruited as a D1 college athlete.

The second most common reaction I get after people hear me repeat this conversation with my coach is, "Are you still angry with him?"

My answer is not at all! Coach Bud saved my life! That conversation prompted me to read, and read, and read some more. I had a lot to prove and little time to prove it! I have found a Bible verse that I apply to this red-letter day of mine: *"Study to show thyself approved unto God, a workman that needed not to be ashamed, rightly dividing the word of truth"* (II Timothy 2:15).

I didn't tell Coach Bud that I was terrible at reading. The reason why I guessed in those tests was because I couldn't keep pace with reading. I couldn't recall concepts when I couldn't read the words or make deeper inferences in passages. I just guessed. I also didn't tell Coach that I was in special education for a reading disability until sixth grade because I was worried he would tell me I didn't qualify, that I was not good enough, that I didn't have the prerequisites, etc. As we would say today, Coach was "just keeping it 100!"

This is how I respond to questions from those who attended my assembly talk. Here is a question for you: Would you say I was college material, with a 2.1 GPA and ITBS (Iowa Tests of Basic Skills) tests scoring in the 60th percentile? My science scores were high because I didn't need reading fluency and comprehension to assess and interpret a graph. My analytical skills were a gift from the Lord, as they stood way out above my other skills. Science and Health were always high-interest areas, and my mind did not categorize them as difficult because they were fun—an interest of mine. Coach didn't know any of these struggles because this was my first time ever being in the student guidance office asking about college. This was the spring of my junior year. This was the first time in my life I was facing emotional pain about school/academic struggles. No matter how heavy or how hard it was, I was determined not to run away from the emotional pain this time. It was hard. I was angry at Coach at first, but I was more determined to face the pain and run toward it. I wasn't giving up the same day I started.

Dear Alice Speraw—your beloved late husband, Coach, and Counselor Bud Speraw saved my life!

Well, my academic and career life, anyway! Am I mad? No way. I am grateful! I thank God for you, Coach Bud. You lit a fire under me that can't be quenched. My friend and brother, Ben Newman, often speaks of "The Burn," a fire deep inside that drives us to attack every day like it's our last. Well, this moment, Brother Ben, is one of my

"Burns" because I continually say to myself, *Son, you are just not college material*, as a catalyst that drives a deep burn in me to talk myself into MOVING toward the uncertainty, then I add: *Study to show yourself approved*. This reminds me of the Burn deep inside me and that I live and attack life for an audience of ONE: Jesus Christ! I stand before you today with four college degrees: two bachelor's degrees from North Dakota State University, a master's degree, and a Ph.D. from the University of Iowa.

Coach Bud, yes, I was deeply hurt and in emotional pain that day, thinking I wasn't college material. Your honesty, which turned into a virtual punch in the mouth, spoke volumes to me. I am a visual learner. Seeing is believing. Showing me those graphs pushed me to face and conquer my emotional pain. Without you speaking truth-in-love to me, I wouldn't have pushed through the pain of my developmental reading disabilities/dyslexia. I read my first book, *The Red Badge of Courage*, in that same spring semester of high school. It was assigned in class, and instead of taking notes in class and taking the test based on my excellent auditory learning skills, I actually read the book and dominated the test!

RESILIENCY HAS FEET; IT'S TIME TO START CLIMBING!

Thank you, Coach Bud Speraw. You are an MVP in my life! May your soul *continue* to rest in full peace knowing you changed my life, the life and legacy of my kids, and the life and legacy of my grandchildren!

9
CONFRONTING LIMITING BELIEFS

INTER-ETHNIC DISCRIMINATION

As an American-born male of Mexican ethnicity, I have longed to feel like I fit in. Not in the sense of fitting into a popular circle, but rather to feel like I belong. As if to say, "Here I am, take me or leave me," except if they left me, I wouldn't feel left out or abandoned.

Unfortunately, I have always been triggered by feelings of rejection and abandonment. My birth father committed suicide when I was a toddler, so there's that. My second book in this three-part series addresses the struggle and the process of healing from "Dad" wounds. Thus, I have been triggered by issues of rejection and abandonment since I can remember, all the way back to Pre-K.

I was having a very difficult time believing that anyone could love me the way Stacey was telling me and showing me. It wasn't that I didn't believe her—she was known for being very sweet, never lying, and being that one trustworthy friend we all wanted. It was that I did not believe I was worthy of such love. That unconditional, unmanipulated, unadulterated love that is a commitment instead of being based on feelings that waver.

Over the years, I have faced discrimination on many fronts. I could almost sense it coming—my body and gut reaction often alerted me before I consciously realized it was becoming a reality. Multiplied over trials, situations, years, and people, this left me with the proverbial chip on my shoulder when it came to these types of triggers.

I worked very hard to surround myself with people I could trust, people who were seemingly battle-tested and stood with me, not against me. My circle was small, and I tended to keep to myself about these "elephant in the room" scenarios around discrimination, bigotry, and racism. The more I showed it to Stacey, the more she asked me if it was happening to us in certain public places when we were together.

People asked us if we realized how extremely difficult it would be to blend two cultures, to work out a mixed-race relationship, and the struggles our child would face being born of a Mexican–Caucasian union. Students our age were often as bad as older adults with hateful comments and statements like, "Date your own kind," "Marry your own race," and "Stay away from our white girls." For the most part, Stacey and I did not fight about this issue until confronted by it in public, which then produced tense conversations about how to manage the outside stress that got injected into our relationship.

We had two scenarios that made us pull away from each other in the form of self-protection. One such situation was when it was obvious that a waitstaff treated me differently than Stacey. Stacey would ask if I felt the same way she did. Once I agreed with her, saying, "Yes, I feel this is discrimination against me," our fight was because she always wanted to call attention to it to confront the staff, management, ownership, etc. I wanted to act as if I was unaware of it because the waitstaff person obviously wanted to disrupt my day and make me feel inadequate or insecure. My goal was twofold: 1) never let that hateful person ruffle my emotions and make me feel like "I have to do something," because I felt like this just played blindly into their hands; 2) if I were to say something to this person who hates me, or to the management or ownership, I was determined to do it after we received our food/products, to ensure there had been no tampering with my food or products! Thus, Stacey would get visibly upset, and my objective was to keep her calm and fly under the radar—then return to key their car later (just kidding!).

People often ask me, "Why would you just ignore it?" My answer is this—I'm not. I am *unoffendable*! Or at least I'm working on becoming *unoffendable*, as my father Jesus lived out his life. The key is the reality that our waitstaff is only exposing the hate in their heart, and it has nothing to do with me! In my third book in this series, you will hear more about having an *unoffendable* heart!

The second scenario that caused us relationship issues was when we were out to eat, and either Stacey was pregnant, or we already had Tyler with us, and some Neanderthals would enter our space and call me names. They used the usual Neanderthal phrases, like "You don't want this" and "You can't handle this," which were easy to ignore. However, when they started calling our son a "half-breed" and/or calling Stacey names about dating (and doing intimate things with) Mexicans, it triggered something in me. My blood boiled, and I found myself standing and walking to the door before I did something that would have me heading back to juvenile detention for fighting again and perhaps being on probation for a second time. Our roles were 100% reversed here. My energy was spiked to shut up these babbling Neanderthals from a rival high school in town. Stacey's energy was in holding me and praying that I would live above the noise, when I was so goal-oriented to stomp out some cockroaches like I did in some of our homes as a kid. To say that this was rare would be a lie. Looking back, I am truly amazed at how well we worked together, even on opposing ends, to keep us focused on us!

INTRA-ETHNIC DISCRIMINATION

This not only happens to me with Caucasian groups but also with brown/Latino groups. As an American-born brown man with Mexican ethnicity, I do not fit in. It feels as if I am forever marginalized.

It has often been said that "Mexican-Americans are too white to be a true Mexican and too brown to truly be an American." There it is: seemingly always squeezed between two groups of people with their life goal to define me—and, in particular, why I am not them.

My entire life has played out this way, causing some trauma that I never knew was there—the underlying engine of my explosive self-protection. When I was in preschool in Iowa, the research on code-switching from one language to another held that one had to master one predominant language prior to learning a second language. Thus, when I would speak in Spanish, I was sent to the corner for a time-out. I learned to associate speaking Spanish with isolation and mental pain.

Interestingly, at my grandma Ruth's house, she would pop me in the mouth when I answered her in English and told me to speak Spanish. So my early childhood language skills were always walking on thin ice. At times, I wanted to speak Spanish simply for the sake of eavesdropping on adult conversations when they spoke Spanish.

However, when my friends were at my house and my grandma spoke in Spanish, I felt wrong, embarrassed, and like I would be punished, so I answered in English and ducked real fast.

When all such matters are taken together, one can see that the limiting beliefs behind one's true actions may not be true at all. Perhaps it's a trap. Perhaps it's a lie. Perhaps they just want to expose your weaknesses. Or perhaps they just want to punish you for being different than them?

HAVE YOU HEARD OF A THOROUGHBRED?

My senior year of football started with a bang. A few games into the fall 1988 season, I was averaging four touchdowns per game. Our team was strong, healthy, and we ran a two-platoon system—offense and defense—to keep everyone rested and fit, with our ultimate goal being a state title. We practiced on a basic field behind the high school, and we all had to walk down a dirt trail to the field. After practice, we had to walk up this terrible hill to get to the high school locker room. On occasion, following a big mistake, the coaches would make someone run the hill as a form of discipline.

One day, I ran that hill a couple of times following a few fumbles in practice. I also got screamed at before and after running the hill. I was usually very mad when this happened, and took it out on the next defender I ran over to score in practice. It was on this day, when I took a break and the second team was running plays, that I noticed something. One running back fumbled and got cussed out, like I did, but never had to run the hill. Yet another running back fumbled and got called a "knucklehead" (as this player was often called) and was just told to "run the play again!" It was at that moment that I realized my head coach might be a racist. I sat back and watched some more, and it was more of the same—dropped passes, fumbles, missed blocks—and yet nobody had to run the hill, especially not twice!

I didn't say anything at the time because I was honestly frozen by the paralysis of analysis. Was it too late to transfer schools? Should I blow the whistle on my coach and the coaching staff and create all this conflict within the team? Should I stuff it down and act like it was all beneath me and just ignore the haters? I also realized in this reflection that it had happened to me a lot last year as a junior running back when I earned the starting job. I thought I ran the hill for every mistake!

I finally asked a friend, and he suggested I go directly to the coach and ask the question to get to the bottom of it. Although it was very scary to consider this choice, it was scarier to disrupt our season and tear our team apart.

I decided to stop by the coach's office before practice one day, and I asked the question. No, it wasn't the question, "Are you a racist?" although that was one of the top two questions I had in mind. Instead, I explained that day in practice and other similar days from hindsight. I asked, "Why do you treat me worse than all the other players?"

One coach asked, "What do you mean?"

I responded, "Why are you harder on me and softer on the other running backs?"

Our head coach/defensive coordinator, Terry, and our offensive coordinator, Coach John Dornan, were at this meeting. Although both were in this meeting, the question was more directed at Coach Dornan because he was my direct coach for the offense and the one who pointed to the hill after a fumble. Coach Dornan had coached our undefeated sophomore team, and I had been his starting running back for three years. He had invited us to his living room on big college football game days and barbequed food for us. I felt close to him, and that's why it cut so deep to feel this way.

Coach Christiansen went first and said something like, "I know how I'm going to respond to this question, but I'll let John go first because you've directed it mostly to him due to the hill running."

Coach Dornan said, "Raúl, have you ever heard of a thoroughbred?"

I said, "A racehorse?"

He said, "Exactly." He went on to share how and why thoroughbreds are bred, raised, trained, and even whipped differently than a typical backyard, family, or farm-work horse.

He asked, "What happens when you come back from the hill?"

"I'm quiet and angry," I replied.

"And how do you play?" he asked.

"I run angry. I run people over."

He said, "You run like a thoroughbred horse with the intention to win!" He went on to talk about how I grow unfocused as practices go on and how I sometimes "take plays off." He said I sometimes would just go through the motions: "You're not really in it fully. So when I see this, and you make a mistake, I send you up the hill." At one point in this discussion, he said, "You run up the hill a boy, and return a man!"

Coach Terry spoke up and talked about what a nice young man I was and offered some positive and kind accolades about me and my choices so far in life. He said that sometimes I play like a "nice young man" instead of a thoroughbred. He mentioned that if they didn't yell at me or get on me, I had a tendency to coast in practice. But in games, I ran like a thoroughbred, and they had to find a way for me to run harder, run angry, and put in 100% effort in practices.

Oddly enough, Coach Terry has a daughter the same age as my son, Tyler, so we talked about that a bit and about those struggles. They had high hopes for me and my future in football, college, and life. It was actually a great meeting.

They eventually asked what I had thought the reason was for them being harder on me than others. I told them, "Because I thought you were racist against me." Coach Terry couldn't believe that I actually said that and believed it. He was emotional and could not believe that I felt that way. I mentioned all the history, all the yelling I got, and all the running I did compared to others. They asked if anyone else believed this, and I mentioned I didn't think so and that it had only started bothering me recently, but in hindsight, the behaviors were there last year, too. Coach Terry was still sad that I thought this about him: he said he worked hard to be a fair and consistent coach. I mentioned that I didn't truly believe it, but I had to know for sure—I had to hear it from both of them.

Coach Dornan was mostly silent during this process. Then he asked, "Did you ever see 'B' run the hill?"

I said, "Yes, but not even close to how many times I ran."

He said, "Exactly, and 'B' is Black—so if I were racist, shouldn't he run as much as you?"

I literally had no words. We sat in silence for a minute, then I just laughed. Then I said, "Good point."

It is absolutely crazy to consider the direct impact this conversation had on my life. It was as if I had won the lottery—the emotional lottery. I was happy, relaxed, and more interested in people who pushed me harder. I was able to press into that uncertainty and fear that almost led me to leave the team, to transfer, or perhaps to quit.

Instead, I saw the world from this perspective: When I am pushed harder by someone close enough to invest in me, then I will run like the thoroughbred I am! This new mindset directly impacted me in all areas of my life. I pushed harder in my life, especially in practice, much to the dismay of my friends on our high school practice field.

Coach Terry Christiansen, you are an MVP in my life and in my development into the man I am today. I value the talks we had about parenting and the times you grabbed me after our co-ed volleyball nights and mentioned to me the skillset to be a dad and a good husband. I know they may have seemed brief and random, but all those pieces of valuable information are bricks I have used to build my life, and I am thankful that I was able to stack them and begin to build my life! Thank you, Coach Christiansen, for being an MVP in my life!

Coach John Dornan, you are an MVP in my life in the way I played football and learned to run out of the snap like a horse out of the gates. Your ability to connect with a broken, trauma-filled young man who did not like male authority because of the double standards they so often represented was a miracle in my life. I met you in tenth grade, and the skills you shared with me were invaluable—from reading the defense to hitting the hole with fervor and to "stick the opponent in the hole."

You were the first person to mention and teach me the "killer instinct" and to never let off the gas "until the fat lady sings." You gave me my opportunity in tenth grade as the starting running back, in 11th grade, and in my senior year. You played such a huge role in helping me fulfill my dream to play college football.

It is because of you that my friends still joke about "Sánchez right and Sánchez left" football plays. You taught me that "There's no better plan than riding the horse that got us to the rodeo" and that if we follow the plan as designed, "It's as easy as shooting fish in a barrel." Oh, we can never forget to "Pin those ears back and play smash-mouth football!" How about, "Walk softly and carry a big stick!" Or the one that brought the most laughs, "It takes a big dog to piss in tall grass!"

The one that sticks out to me the most, perhaps because it echoes my grandma Ruth, is "There is no excuse for not going 100 percent!" Finally, I can't thank you enough for that very hard conversation that led us all to cry, then to hug it out, and finish with laughter!

Coaches truly carry the light of the world and make the Lord smile with a joyful heart, as your light lit me up and all the players who knew you. THANK YOU, Coach John Dornan, for being an MVP in my life, my launch, and my living legacy! May your soul forever rest in peace.

10

SUMMARY: MOVING TOWARD UNCERTAINTY

As you recall, Strong's G3326 states that Transform is translated from "metamorphoō"—to change into another form, to transform, to transfigure. "Renewing," "anakaninōsis," means a renewal, renovation, a complete change for the better. "Mind," "nous" (nooce), means the intellect, i.e., mind (divine or human; in thought, feeling, or will); by implication, meaning:—mind, understanding. Also, the capacity for spiritual truth, the higher powers of the soul, the faculty of perceiving divine things, of recognizing goodness, and of hating evil. Thus, we are metamorphosing into another form, a renewed you, with more and stronger capacity to be stretched, to carry more stress, more opportunity, and to MOVE to your new normal, your next level.

In this MOVE section of this book, we could see multiple scenarios where hiding from the truth seemed easy, comfortable, and even welcoming. In the simplest form, it's like an old shoe. It's so comfy and yet so old, worn-out, and incapable of carrying you for another mile! However, new shoes, no matter how cool they look, do not yet fit like they're made for you—it's just so much easier to stay stuck in the comfort zone of pain because it's predictable.

My goal for you is to RUN! Never forget that your comfort zone is a trap. It has been said that "the comfort zone is where goals go to die."

It's true. Never forget that the truth sets you free, and the comfort zone imprisons you in the past.

We learned that MOVING is the key to success.

It is important to see the transformation. The first major transformation was Stacey's ability to let go of her own fear, her own pain, and her own feeling of loss.

She was a star cheerleader and wasn't able to cheer for one full year. During most of her pregnancy, she wasn't able to sit at a desk facing forward; she had to sit in the desk facing sideways. People not only didn't go out of their way to help her, but some even teased her—until I put a stop to it as soon as possible.

And yet, in the midst of her personal struggles and pain, she was always ready to help me with my emotional pains so that I wouldn't climb back into the hole and put on my armor of self-protection.

For me, the light switch that got turned on was the metamorphosis of movement. I was pushing into uncertainty. This newfound movement was most certainly due to a natural instinct to protect. I was protecting Stacey physically and emotionally, and this allowed me to believe that I could protect and parent our child as well.

I was learning to connect to a deep drive to not infect my son with the deep pain of abandonment. I had to prove that I am *not* my father; I am *not* my stepfather. I *am* Tyler's father, and I will make him proud of me!

It is in this section of the book where the rubber truly meets the road. There was a lot of talk about me going to college and playing college football. There was a lot of talk about me being one of the top cooks at my grandmother's restaurant, even at 16 and 17 years old. There was a lot of talk about me being a renewed man.

I was learning how to make attempts and not quit due to failures, falling short of the goal, or even doing great and still losing in team sports. I was learning that resiliency has feet and that I needed to keep moving no matter the circumstances.

Keep moving.

Keep climbing.

Keep attacking.

Keep stacking those bands of resilience of successive attempts toward your goal. It is here that one learns consistency, momentum, habits, and how to attack the routine to develop a *Resilient Mind* that never allows the trash of circumstances, environment, public ridicule, or public opinion to ruin my climb to greatness. I will be a great dad!

I was learning how to set goals and how to move into the uncertainty of my new life endeavors, and yet the old pain was still coming back, turned on as if with a light switch. Again, I did not control the light switch; it was on or off based on triggers, situations, emotional pain, life circumstances, and, yes, sometimes my own anger.

However, the ability to lock down repetitive, successive attempts at any new normal behavior is the only way to create resiliency, and it was working.

There's no better joy than knowing that the goal I set is now my reality.

There's no better feeling than knowing my son is watching me and learning my new habits as fast as I am laying them down.

There's no better feeling than knowing my girlfriend is learning to trust me, loves me, and feels proud of my progress.

There is no better acceptance than knowing I can be proud of myself—if even for a moment, if even for a single situation or achievement. Yes, I may cheer for myself even if no one else seemed to care.

In the beginning, I wanted to be great, and that meant being very successful, being talked about, carrying some pride, and having people talk about my success. Rather quickly, Stacey was helping me see that greatness in the Kingdom of God is serving and not bragging.

She often talked about humility, and I paired humility with being vulnerable, being weak, and basically being a victim. I now know that that's not the truth. The ability to be humble in front of our Lord and Savior, to be humble in front of my girlfriend, to be humble in front of my son, and really opened up my emotional life. I had more joy; I had more fun.

I was learning how to pray for my enemies. I would pray for people who cursed at me at a restaurant. I was trying to become more like Stacey, as she was trying to be more like Jesus.

My mentors, my coaches, and those who lit a deep burn in me to go deeper, and to push harder, allowed me to realize there is more in me, and the harder I push, the deeper I can get. It is also amazing to know that a 17-year-old was pushed into the uncertainty of confronting coaches, counselors, and mentors.

Thankfully, I was wrong in each of those cases, and they were humble enough to continue to help me, work with me, cheer me on, and guide me all the way to hit my goals and to be standing here today teaching you.

Being transformed by the renewing of your mind is not hiding, it's not avoiding, it's not going around the barrier. It's literally driving right through the detour and discovering the answer for yourself.

It is this truth that truly sets one free. That 100-pound weight vest unzipped and dropped to the ground when I realized Coach Bud Speraw was just keeping it 100; when I realized that Coach Terry and Coach John were literally pushing me differently because they saw me as a thoroughbred and not just another horse in the race.

For you, what are you currently trying to go around? What are you currently afraid of? What are you currently hiding from? By whom do you feel threatened or discriminated against? Who has stopped your climb to your next level of greatness?

Yes, take some time right now, grab a pen, and write it down. Circle it. Highlight it, and ask yourself this question: "Who will I become when I push into this detour of *uncertainty* and shed the pains of the past?

If I were talking to you right now, you would tell me that you were afraid of failing, or that you were afraid of being rejected, or afraid of not being good enough. But I'd tell you that's a lie. You're lying to yourself because you've never seen behind the detour before.

I need you, right now, to close your eyes and see yourself pushing through the barrier as if you have a 4x4 armored truck. See your answer and realize that all you need is already in you. You're literally afraid of being great—the greatness of serving others, the greatness of setting people free from their emotional pain, the greatness of serving our Lord and Savior Jesus Christ, the greatness of doing the work of the Gospel of Jesus Christ. The greatness of knowing that the harvest is plentiful, but the laborers are few.

I need you to go stack those bands of resilience as fast as you can.

Resilient Mind

Never forget that resiliency has feet, so you have to walk out your own climb, walk through your own barriers, walk through your own detours, and get the tough answers that you have been afraid of. Once you have been set free, you are free indeed.

This is the only way you can drop your limiting beliefs because your limiting beliefs always hide behind a detour. And although it seems easier and faster to take the scenic route and go around it, there's no true greatness in hiding from yourself. There's only a dark closet of self-protection. Never ever forget:

"There's

**To Be Great: When You Feel Like It
And When You Don't!"**™

PART III

FINDING WHAT'S AWESOME ABOUT THAT (WAAT)

I) And be not conformed to this world,
(II) but be ye transformed by the renewing of your mind,
(III) that ye may prove what is that good, and acceptable, and perfect, will of God.
(Romans 12:2) KJV

Action step III: FIND WAAT Moment(s) in Every Situation!

"Fill the earth with your songs of gratitude."
— Charles Spurgeon

11

LET GO TO GROW

Come on now! The self-protection mindset ready to protect and hide itself at all costs doesn't just depart of its own volition! You need to shed it off yourself continually until it's gone for good! In one of these wounded times, Stacey taught me my mantra, a song by Carl Vaughan that I still use to this day.

I cannot be defeated, and I will not quit
Been redeemed by the blood of Jesus, released from Satan's pit
Jesus fought, and he won the battle, and he gave it all to me
I cannot be defeated! I'm saved, I'm healed, I'm FREE![1]

Self-awareness is a key to life because it gets you to stop and take a different perspective on any situation. This mantra allowed me to see my situation and still stay in my own lane. While standing in the same shoes of being offended, I could consider a different emotional attachment to the scenario. Having a different emotional attachment meant my first reaction wasn't truly *me*. I mean, if I can let an attachment go and instantly pick up another one, it means I'm not *intrinsically attached* to it. This means I can let it go. I can shed it away from me. I can

---

1. Copeland, Kenneth. "I Cannot Be Defeated." *The Kenneth Copeland Collection Volume 1*. KCP Records, 2005.

detach. It is here—when we detach—that we truly feel free! Freedom cannot be bought. It can only be achieved via the mind. Freedom isn't a position, a place, a time, or a space. Freedom is a mindset where I am free from whatever it was that emotionally attached to me and made me feel like I had to respond in a similar emotional fashion as in the past. I was offended, so I must either react and re-offend or go hide to self-protect.

Once I started singing, I was able to detach and drop the yoke around my neck. The old habits I learned from being raised a certain way, of managing anger a certain way. The *programmed habit* for me was attacking when I felt attacked. Wow! This cannot be overstated. When you truly shed those behaviors on your own terms, you truly are free—*"And whom Christ sets free is free indeed"* (John 8:36).

This newfound freedom in perception allows you to realize how long you have been imprisoned by your own emotions and fear of pain to your own perception. Only in walking completely through the pain can you see that it isn't truly you. It is what happened to you. You can choose to carry these experiences and choices as a badge of honor —like time spent in a mental prison—or as a history of pain and failure, justifying why you cannot succeed. Or, you can shed them like the dead weight they are and move toward freedom, which only comes by confronting and accepting the pain. This occurs by intentionally walking through the pain and then shedding all of it except for the lesson learned. From there, when that old pain gets triggered, you will only bring up the one lesson learned, that What's Awesome About That (WAAT moment) from the pain—and this, my friend, is your new *Resilient Mind!*

"WHAT IF?"

What if it is not about what our Lord allows in our life? Or what if it isn't about a feeling, like I did something right to deserve this, or that I did something wrong to deserve that? Instead, what if it is always about how our Lord provides? Our Lord always provides a way out for us when we are stuck. He always provides a source of comfort when we are downcast. He always provides a way to grow, even when it seems impossible to keep going. What if our Lord is continually moving us on, precept upon precept and line upon line (Proverbs 28:10)? This mindset is the set-up for you to win. This mindset says that no matter what, the Lord has a plan for you.

What if this plan is set out for us in Romans 12:2?

> *"And be not conformed to this world: but be ye transformed by the renewing of your mind, that ye may prove what is that good, and acceptable, and perfect, will of God."*
> (Romans 12:2)

Our goal is to *Renew* your perspective. *Move* toward uncertainty. Then, *Find* what is awesome about that (WAAT) in the midst of your current struggle. What if this was our purpose: *Renew, Move,* and *Find*?

In every circumstance of life, even in those that are life-altering (having a child at 17 and 16 years old), what if we stopped asking, "Why was this allowed?" and instead asked, "Where is the Hand of God?" This is a simple change in our questions, but it makes the difference between a life that gets buried in the "Why" and collects hardships, pain, and regret upon regret or a life that reboots with the "Where" question that sparks a climb of Renewing, Moving, and Finding.

In my opinion, it is this "Where" question that gets me off the sidelines and into the game. In football, we can only score points when we possess the ball—regardless of whether we're on offense or defense!

This is also true in life. We can only score points when we ask the right question. The ability to own our thoughts begins with the right question: not *why,* but *where?*

Our self-awareness is always rooted in the *answer* we choose. "Why did the Lord allow this?" means I will be standing on answers that keep the focus on my past. Answers will always move you. It is up to you to determine if you want to continue moving backward in self-protection mode, being conformed to the patterns of the past—accepting your own mental prison as your destiny. Or you can choose to move forward toward the uncertainty, the fear, and the pain to gain a new awareness that the closer you get to the root, the more clearly you will see that it was a whole lot of smoke and mirrors. Yes, it's scary! Yes, it isn't fun. And yes, it unlocks my mental prison and opens a new path to a new destiny.

"Why did we not use a condom?" This question kept me stuck in the past, looking for answers that my mom wanted when I told her the news. "Why did we not have adult supervision at my friend's house, and why were we left alone?" Those were the answers that Fran wanted. Answering these questions was not a problem. Getting stuck on them was definitely a problem.

In six months of dating, we never needed a condom because I was waiting on her. Stacey also trusted that I didn't carry a condom, nor was I planning on needing one. I was working to become a new person. My old ways were gone or at least had an eviction notice. I wasn't initiating any intimacy and had worked hard on staying within the boundaries Stacey set in place for us. However, on that one night, I wasn't prepared for her to initiate intimacy.

The best lesson of all that I have taught over the past 37 years is one word: Yes! Yes, it is entirely possible to get pregnant the first time! There it is, and that is that.

The questions that we ponder, but fail to answer, pin us into a mental prison of the past. The questions that we answer honestly release us into our new perspective that drives us to new levels of **Renewing, Moving,** and **Finding**!

12

CHASING DOWN THE DREAM

I continued working at Ruth's Cosina. Stacey continued working at Orange Julius. We continued dating with the knowledge that she would probably go to Springfield, Missouri, to Evangel College, and I would go play college football somewhere else. I continued in track, baseball, and football. I gave up organized basketball to work and get bigger, faster, stronger. It was our senior year and it was time to shine.

(Raúl (18) and Tyler (10 months), our senior picture)

I went to the University of Iowa and the University of Nebraska football camps in the summer of 1988, before my senior year at high school. I did very well, and they both recruited me. Coach Bill Snyder from the University of Iowa gave me a couple phone calls and sent me several letters. Coach Ron Brown, from the University of Nebraska, called me every Friday night after my football games and would ask me two questions: "Did you stay healthy?" and "How many YACs (yards after contact) did you have?" We talked for ten minutes, and he always finished with, "God bless you!" I always thought I would go to Nebraska. They were my first choice. They rank all the athletes at their football camp each year on a unitary scale. That year I was ranked #13 out of all their 300+ campers.

After my football games, Stacey and I rushed to the drive-through or stopped in to say a quick hello to our friends at McDonalds. Then we rushed home for my call from Coach Ron Brown. After the call, Stacey and I began talking about the possibility of going to college together as a family and what that would look like.

(Raúl (18), Stacey (17), and Tyler (10 months) before our senior year Homecoming)

My five official visits were to the University of Iowa, the University of Nebraska, Iowa State University, the University of Northern Iowa, and North Dakota State University. I picked big games on their schedules to see the atmosphere and to feel the big game day energy. I was present for the Iowa vs Michigan game that ended in a tie. I witnessed the University of Nebraska kill Arizona State.

I lived vicariously at the Iowa State vs. Oklahoma State game. I got to see College Football and Pro Football Hall of Famer Barry Sanders play live. He was lightning in the form of a human! He rolled up ISU for about 293 yards and 4 TDs. I enjoyed watching and studying Barry Sanders. When I got my hands on the 1988 *BFS Magazine* article on him, I liked it so much that I ripped it out of the magazine and taped it to my wall at home. I tried to emulate him in anything that I had the capability to climb toward. He set goals in everything, for practice, for games, for his seasons, and in life. It helped me to start looking not just to football to climb to new goals but in my daily life, too.

At my ISU visit, I took along Stacey's dad, Jerry Fish. At the pregame activities, I left the ISU end zone, where the Cyclone running backs were running drills, and walked to the other end zone where Barry Sanders and the Cowboy running backs were running theirs. I simply could not believe my eyes. He was even bigger in person. The phrase "tree trunks for legs" doesn't do him justice. He could side-step five yards! It was just unreal. I understand how this may sound, but I partly used ISU to see Barry in person. I wanted a full ride to ISU football, but Sanders was my hero!

THE FLEECE

Prior to my official visits, I had laid out a fleece, like a deal with God. All I knew was that I was in love with Stacey and didn't know what to do next. I didn't want to abandon my childhood dream of getting a full ride to play college football. We didn't know how to proceed into college life as a couple. We were in love now and no longer just co-parents who were dating. In my prayer time, I asked for a sign from God. During my official college visits, I asked that the good Lord *show me* the way by having *only one* school acknowledge that they cared not just for me as an athlete but also for me as a father and perhaps a married man.

My official visit to NDSU was postponed due to bad weather, and it was moved to January of 1989. It was my last official visit. It was their National Championship Banquet weekend from the perfect 1988 NDSU Bison season. Even though I wasn't engaged yet, I told all the schools that I had a son, and it was a strong possibility that I would go to college as a married man with a son.

Interestingly, one college completely forgot to take me on a tour of married student housing. Three colleges had a spot on the itinerary for me to go visit the Married Student Housing "on my own" time, or they said that I could go tour it after our official football visit.

ONLY North Dakota State University had a spot on the itinerary for me to go visit married student housing, even during their busy weekend National Championship Banquet activity. My recruiting coach, Bruce Saum, had asked a married family if they would do a campus housing walk-through with me. When we arrived and drove to the married student housing complex on the NDSU campus, they were expecting us. We walked through their townhome, and I asked them questions. I felt very comfortable with the notion that NDSU knew I was coming as a married man with a son. It was inspiring to see that they were comfortable with it as well.

It is always the spiritual world that matters. It really wasn't about what the married student housing actually looked like. It was 100% an act of obedience. I asked God to *show me*, and I promised I would go! People have these decisions so twisted. Obedience isn't at all about slavery or being weak or using a relationship with Christ as a crutch in difficult seasons.

Obedience always is and always will be about living with 100% freedom in Christ Jesus. It is only in my obedience to my relationship with God that I am 100% FREE! I asked God to tell me that *only one* school would have my "dad" and "husband" goals in mind, and He came through! I wasn't abandoned! I wasn't rejected or forgotten! He never left me, and He was the light on my feet and my path (Psalm 119:105).

The 100% freedom we sensed came in knowing that God heard my cry, answered me, and walked before me to prepare *our* way to North Dakota State University (NDSU)! I did not actually hear the Lord tell me that out loud, but I felt it in my spirit. I was to hold out for the school that showed me their married student housing.

People who hear our story have asked, "What if none of the schools had shown you the married housing?" I have said, "I don't know. It never crossed my mind that He would not provide!" I always tell people with those questions, "I guess I am naive enough to believe God at His word!"

My job was to fully commit to NDSU and a full-ride football scholarship offer as a married man with a son! Oh, and by the way, this was via my goal and promise to myself after my tenth-grade football season to gain 50 lbs. in two years. I successfully climbed all the way to my goal. I had started at 155 lbs. I was a 205 lbs. high school senior running back with a 4.55-second 40-yard dash speed (when clocked at the U of Nebraska football camp, the electronic time was 4.75 two times in a row).

After committing to NDSU, I asked Stacey to become my wife, and she said yes! We got married the summer after we graduated from high school in 1989. This is her story to tell, as the engagement story seems to have taken on a life of its own! Yes, I owe you, Stacey, as it was not the way you dreamed it would be on the day you said "YES" for life.

We won the Iowa Shrine All-Star Football game. I was a running back for the North, and our starting quarterback was none other than the Hall Of Famer from "The Greatest Show on Turf," Kurt Warner! That was a great game, and we won with a game-winning drive to secure the victory over the South. I had my bachelor party that night. Sunday night was our rehearsal dinner. Monday night, we were married, July 31st, 1989! Wow, she is gorgeous, and she is my bride for life!

The three of us went to NDSU together as a family: two 18-year-old newlyweds, new co-parents to an 18-month-old son. We were both freshmen chasing a bachelor's degree, all alone as a family up in Fargo, North Dakota. I was a "rook" on the National Champion NDSU BISON football team. Yes, you may exhale now. This is all part of the process of becoming refined by fire to developing a *Resilient Mind* by renewing, moving, and finding!

(Raúl living his reality at NDSU playing college football as a married man and a father!)

People always ask me, "What is your secret sauce to success?" My answer will never change. "My Lord and Savior Jesus Christ." He paid all my past and future debts to free me from myself—from my *mental prison*! And my mantra since I was a young teen has been, *"I will not be broken!"* After Stacey taught me that song, I added: *"I cannot be defeated!"* At 18 years of age and accepting Jesus Christ as my Lord and Savior, I realized, *"If God is for me, then who can be against me."*

I literally say these on repeat when I catch myself wanting to hide from the pain instead of suiting up to kick butt and take names. It reminds me that my life was bought at a price. It is not mine to go hide in storage. The Bible states it this way:

*"No one, when he hath lighted a candle, putteth it in a secret place,
neither under a bushel, but on a candlestick,
that they which come in may see the light."*
(Luke 11:33)

Believe me when I tell you that this self-talk and knowing that my savior is *for me* is my secret to success!

13

FINDING THE HAND OF GOD

Finding is a learned skillset. It's an acquired skill because it has a delayed reward. Just because you set out to find something is never a guarantee that you will indeed find it. It is here that you embark on a journey to look back and find that *"good, acceptable, and perfect will of God."*

This is especially true of the Hand of God. If you find it, how will you know it is truly him? How can you know? What is your next move when you find it? What do you tell people? Will they even believe you? Are Christians more or less willing to believe you? Will you get upgraded with God, like on *The Amazing Race*, when you bring back the gold ticket?

These are only the tip of the iceberg for why people do and do not set out to find the Hand of God because it is here that one may grasp an assignment for oneself and feel—even if for a moment in time—that God actually and literally sees me, cares for me, assigned me, is willing to use me: "Here am I, Lord. Send me!"

And yet, like almost every other delayed gratification, most who embark on the climb throw in the towel. Most surrender their dream, life goal, their calling because they haven't seen progress; haven't heard from the Lord; feel like they are moving in circles; feel like they can identify their cycles through phases of approach and avoidance, and then quitting.

In our story, we walked out two separate climbs. Stacey was looking for the Hand of God with her parents. Meanwhile, I was merely trying to wrap my head around the concept of Jesus. I grew up with my Aunt Gerri, who took me to her church, Bethel Baptist, in Sioux City, IA. I felt like I understood—or at least wanted to—the concept of God. I know I felt like I could feel His presence at times, as I recall a handful of times when I couldn't sleep and was prompted to pray for someone in particular as a child and middle schooler.

Listed below are the significant pillars of spiritual strength that poured into me throughout my life. It is crazy to look back and see the *Hand of God* in each of these early childhood, early teenage years, and early college years. When you learn how to Renew, Move, and Find, one can truly be unbreakable. This isn't a form of pride. It is a surrender to that all-knowing, all-sufficient, omnipotent, and omnipresence of the *Hand of God*, the only true living God, *YHWY!*

Let us go back and revisit my "in loving memory" list of saints in my life, listed chronologically of when they impacted my life/our life:

> In loving memory of
> Aunt Gerri
> Ruth Castillo
> Margret & Leo Fish
> Valencia & Ray Fife
> Aunt Margaret Heiland (Peg)
> Fran Fish

Thank you, Aunt Gerri. Knocking on my door and windows early Sunday mornings to *"get my butt to ssshhhrrrch"* was a pain. However, it did set the tone for me to hear the word of the Lord at Awana Club. You were sent by God on assignment to set the foundation of God to allow me to hear Stacey's message about Jesus. The Dunkin Donuts were undefeated, too!

Thank you, Grandma Ruth. Your tough love built me, and your skilled work ethic developed me. You were truly my first resiliency coach: "Ahh, it's just a burn. It will teach you to move faster (in the kitchen)." After you dedicated your life to Jesus, our very serious talks about generational curses, bloodline covenants, and how to stand in the gap for our family tree set a BURN in me to lead and set the captives free from mental prisons!

Thank you, Aunt Peg (Margret), for the years of monthly financial support and prayers for us while in college. A little goes a long way when one is broke. The "diaper money" saved us in college.

Thank you, Grandma Valencia, for loving me and praying over me. Thank you, Grandpa Ray, for our conversations about the Biblical views on race, ethnicity, and culture and the power of the Jesus Culture. I wish we could have had more time together.

Thank you, Grandma Margaret, for loving me and praying over me. I always appreciated you serving me and telling me stories about Jerry that were not so godly.

Thank you, Grandpa Leo, for all our hunting and free-range organic protein talks that you seamlessly weaved into scriptural talks. Thank you for immediately accepting me on day 1–Thanksgiving day 1986, on the farm, in the very beginning of dating your granddaughter Stacey. I was never an in-law to you, and this helped heal wounds from my mental prison.

Thank you, Fran (Frannie Fran Fran). Your ability to love me, my story, and intimately attempt to understand my past was essential to me developing a relationship with Jesus Christ. We had fun racing to complete your brain puzzles, which I was certain you had practiced beforehand. I was never an in-law to you, and this acceptance rescued me emotionally!

14

SUMMARY: FINDING WHAT'S AWESOME ABOUT THAT (WAAT)

> "...that ye may *prove* what is that good, and acceptable, and perfect, will of God."
> (Romans 12:2)

Asking someone to look back at the thing that used to scare them and purposefully look for a WAAT moment can seem downright rude at first. However, not asking someone to do this task is literally being guilty by association. It's like being the driver in a get-away car—you are enabling the crime of keeping someone locked up in their own *mental prison*.

Let's take a look back and see the Hand of God in the areas that caused us so much mental pain.

First, I was coasting in my life, with the exception of sports performance, as I assumed one could get into college based only on athletic skills. Becoming a teen dad at 17 catapulted my academic achievement for the purpose of making my son proud of me and to get a scholarship to college to play football.

Second, having a son at 17 pushed me into my *mental prison* at such an early age that it became a skillset that the Lord has allowed me to make into my profession. I learned very quickly that the old habits never die; they must be suffocated! The ability to renew, move, and find was something I was living out loud. I was actively attacking the pain points because I wanted to be healthy for my son. I was able to keep seeking help, support, and finding that on the other end of the pain is freedom, knowledge, and power. The power to change. The power to forgive. The power to let go and grow. The power to accept! I accepted love, forgiveness, pain, suffering for a purpose, healing, and salvation through Jesus Christ's death and resurrection.

Third, I was able to love. Loving a son is something you cannot teach—it is an experience! I often tell teens when I speak, "I would not wish being a teen dad on anyone, and I would personally do it all over again if I had the choice." This usually dumbfounds people. They say, "Isn't that a contradiction?" Perhaps, from the outside looking in it does. However, from my perspective of WAAT moments, it literally is a match made in Heaven. The things my son, Tyler, taught me are priceless. He taught me that nothing is that big of a deal. He taught me that everything is funny: farts, burps, boogers, poopy diapers, peeing, and missing the mark, all of it. I was able to renew my own childhood via his. I was able to begin to heal all my dad wounds by being a dad. I literally cry out of gratitude that the Lord would entrust me with such a precious soul. I am in awe of the plan of the Lord.

The Bible states:

"For I know the plans I have for you," declares the Lord, "plans to prosper you and not to harm you, plans to give you hope and a future."
(Jerimiah 29:11 KJV)

Again, I am not asking "why" this happened with Stacey and me. I am asking, "Where was the hand of the Lord?" I see that whatever was meant for evil—teen pregnancy, poverty, failure, etc.—the good Lord God Almighty turned it into good! No, I am not saying this was His plan for us from the beginning. Yes, I am saying that Stacey and I shut off our GPS and took a scenic route and, as only the good Lord can do, He redeemed us—*"But God commendeth his love toward us, in that, while we were yet sinners, Christ died for us"* (Romans 5:8 KJV).

Knowing Christ's love for me and Stacey's love for me allowed me to love back. Loving our son Tyler was easy—he was such a lovable, fun, energetic, athletic, and smart child. My ability to love Stacey and Tyler was directly related to my ability to accept love from the Lord and Stacey. My WAAT moments in these areas alone are still paying ginormous ROI's.

Fourthly, having a crib in my room allowed me to see a daily visual aid that I am no longer living for myself. It isn't about me any longer—it is about us. Yes, it was hard to navigate. Will Stacey be with me? Will we have to "team-parent"? Will we have to live a long-distance relationship? I lived by climbing so hard that my hope was that I would attract Stacey to follow me. This ability to live for someone or something outside of oneself is huge. It cannot be overstated. It is most often understated. I think the notion that I am living for us was the chronic visual aid I needed to stay on my climb and to never look back, to never give up, to never surrender. This was one of my greatest supports—seeing Tyler's crib was a daily reminder of the question: "Did you do enough today to climb out?" Some days, laying in bed, looking at his crib, and asking this question, I would get out of bed and lift weights in my room late at night, even to 1 am. It drove me hard. I am very thankful for that drive. I don't think I would have driven so hard without the knowledge that I am living for us now.

Lastly, there is the WAAT moment about how NDSU happened. I mean, the fleece, the Championship weekend official visit, the married student housing itinerary that no other school had done—not even close. Coach Bruce Saum went above and beyond his coaching duties to personally escort an 18-year-old young man with a one-year-old son. He also assisted me with the entire married student housing after I committed to NDSU, so we had housing organized when we started football in early August, prior to the normal time incoming students typically arrive on campus.

What a beginning to our Living Legacy: my Living Legacy of Stacey and Tyler on a dream journey with me to play college football on a National Championship Team. As you can see, I am not a self-made man. Frankly, any person claiming to be self-made is highly likely lying to you. Nobody achieves anything alone. After all, one needs clients, customers, buyers, etc. Nobody is self-made, not even

Jesus! Jesus was continually challenged by our Abba Father, who—through prayer and divine intervention—continued to empower Jesus to do what Jesus did.

As we reflect back to the earlier chapters in this book, it is my sincere hope that you can see that I am not saying I am self-made. In fact, my hope is that you see:

I was broken, and then I was whole

I wanted to run, then I stayed to fight the good fight of faith

I wanted to hide from the pain and hope it would just all work out

I tried my best to push Stacey, the Bible, and Jesus away from me, then learned to accept her, the Bible, and my Jesus!

What is awesome about that (WAAT) is that I learned I am enough; I am loved; I am wanted; I am accepted; I am not my mistakes; I am not my biological dad or my genetic code; I am not my stepfather figures; I am who the Lord God Almighty says I am! I am fearfully and wonderfully made. I am the Lord's masterpiece. I am the clay, and He is the potter. I am saved by grace!

Finally, it is my prayer that the concepts in this book resonate with you to push into the pain of your past by RENEWING your perspective, *MOVING Toward Uncertainty*, and FINDING what's awesome about that (WAAT) in every situation.

If you liked this book, please be on the lookout next year for my second offering in this series: *The Secret Process of Renewing Your Mind: RESILIENT DAD*. It walks through the Renew, Move, and Find steps of being a congruent dad—even if you never had a congruent dad to teach you how.

If you liked this book, you may also like our podcast at: Renewing the Mind Podcast, available on YouTube, iTunes, Spotify, and wherever you find your favorite podcasts. You can also find our Living Legacy Coaching programs on our website at: www.drraulsanchez.com.

Resilient Mind

Never ever forget:

"There's

To Be Great: When You Feel Like It
And When You Don't!"™

THANK YOU FOR READING MY BOOK!

DOWNLOAD YOUR FREE GIFTS

Just to say thanks for buying and reading my book, I would like to give you a free inspirational video to get a jump on your climb. You may also join our free community to be included in our movement!

Scan the QR Code Here:

I appreciate your interest in my book and value your feedback as it helps me improve future versions of this book. I would appreciate it if you could leave your invaluable review on Amazon.com with your feedback. Thank you!

www.ingramcontent.com/pod-product-compliance
Lightning Source LLC
Chambersburg PA
CBHW032049090426
42744CB00004B/134